Comprehension Cliffhanger Stories

15 Action-Packed Stories That Invite Students to Infer, Visualize, and Summarize to Predict the Ending of Each Story

by Tom Conklin

SCHOLASTIC
PROFESSIONAL BOOKS

NEW YORK • TORONTO • LONDON • AUCKLAND • SYDNEY
MEXICO CITY • NEW DELHI • HONG KONG • BUENOS AIRES

Cover design by Norma Ortiz
Cover art by Jim Caputo
Interior design by Solutions by Design, Inc.

ISBN: 0-439-15978-4

8 9 10   40   09 08 07 06

Table of Contents

Introduction

The high-interest stories in this book were written to help your students improve their reading skills and promote a love of reading. In each story, there is a point at which students should stop reading and make predictions about how the story will end. You may want to read the first story aloud to model for students the thinking and reflection that this stopping point allows for.

Each story includes a companion teacher page that provides a list of vocabulary words. You may want to review these words with students before they read. The Before Reading section includes suggestions for building background and helping students to focus on a particular reading strategy. Some of the reading strategies include:

- Making Predictions

- Understanding Cause and Effect

- Making Inferences

- Visualizing

- Summarizing

- Understanding Genre

- Understanding Literary Elements

- Reading for Details

After they've read the story, encourage discussion and writing by using the prompts in the After Reading section.

"The Cliffhanger"

Before Reading

BUILDING BACKGROUND

Tell students that this story is about kids who go rock climbing. Ask students if they have seen rock climbers on television or in movies. Many fitness centers offer rock climbing as an activity. Let students who have seen or tried rock climbing describe the activity.

READING STRATEGY FOCUS: MAKING PREDICTIONS

Ask students what they think of when they hear the word "cliffhanger." Break the compound word into its two root words, "cliff" and "hanger."

Point out that "cliffhanger" is a term used to describe a certain type of story. Ask students what sort of story they would expect a cliffhanger to be.

After Reading

TALK ABOUT IT

Discuss with students how Andy, Tierney, and Pat got into their predicament. Ask for words to describe Andy's state of mind when he decided to try climbing the cliff. Elicit that Andy was over-confident.

Ask students to think of a time they may have been overconfident. Let volunteers describe their own stories—how they were overconfident and what the results were.

WRITE ABOUT IT

Let students write a short story or skit showing a character who is overconfident.

VOCABULARY

Here are words your students will encounter in this story, along with their appropriate meanings:

boulders—large, roundish stones

cinched—held tight

commanded—ordered with authority

confident—sure of oneself, bold

device—a gadget

exhaustion—extreme tiredness

explorers—people who travel to make discoveries

fingertips—the ends of one's fingers

focused—concentrated on

glinted—shined off of

gnarled—twisty

jutting—sticking out

lurch—make a sudden, sharp movement

scrambled—moved quickly

squinting—looking through half-closed eyes

towering—standing far above

whimpering—using a quiet, crying tone

5

"The Cliffhanger"

○ ○ ○ ○ ○ ○ ○ ○ ○ ○ ○

Andy was clinging with his bare hands to a rock wall. One hundred feet below him, boulders were scattered on the hard ground.

○ ○ ○ ○ ○ ○ ○ ○ ○ ○ ○

"Don't worry! We'll make it to the top!" Andy's voice was confident, but his heart was beating hard with fear.

Andy was clinging with his bare hands to a rock wall. One hundred feet below him, boulders were scattered on the hard ground. Andy blinked the sweat from his eyes and looked up. The edge of the cliff was about ten feet above his head. It may as well have been a mile.

Andy stole a look down. His two friends, Tierney and Pat, were hanging by their fingertips beneath him. A single rope attached the three climbers. Andy moved his left hand a few inches. Dirt gave away under his fingers. He clawed at the cliff wall, somehow grabbing hold as pebbles and clods of earth rattled down the rock wall.

"Are you all right?" Tierney gasped.

"I'm hanging in there," Andy called back, trying to force a smile. He looked up again. Andy spied a gnarled tree root jutting from the cliff wall, about two feet beneath the top of the cliff. If he could only make it to the root, then he could pull them all to safety....

One hour earlier, danger had been the farthest thing from Andy's mind. All he could think about then was lunch.

Andy, Tierney, and Pat had been on an early morning hike through Yosemite National Park. The three friends were there on a camping trip with Andy's family. Andy's little brother, Ian, had made a pest of himself all morning long, begging to tag along with Andy and the others.

"Take your brother with you," Andy's dad had said, as the campers cleaned up after their breakfast.

"But, Dad," Andy whined, "we're going to go exploring in the canyon. We can't have a little kid tag along when we go rock-climbing."

"That's where you're wrong!" Andy's mom chimed in. "I don't want you

6

kids climbing any rocks that are too steep for Ian to handle."

"And be back before one," added Ian's dad. "Show up later than that, and you'll miss lunch."

Now, lunch was the last thing on Andy's mind. The bright sunlight glinted off the face of his watch as he inched his hand up the wall. He spied the watch's hands. It was ten after one. So much for lunch, Andy thought.

A half hour earlier, after spending the morning trooping across the hot, sun-baked ground in the canyon, the four explorers found themselves more than halfway home. As they passed into the cool shadows under the cliff, Andy looked up.

"Isn't that the tree that's about a half mile from our camp?" he asked, pointing to a tall pine towering over the edge of the cliff.

"Looks like it," Pat said, squinting at the sky.

"Great!" Andy said. "We can save at least a half hour by climbing up the side of the wall instead of going all the way on the path."

"No way!" little Ian yelped as he stared up the cliff. "I wouldn't climb that wall with a ladder!"

"Don't be chicken," Andy said as he prepared the ropes for their climb.

"I don't know," Tierney said, looking up the wall. "Ian may be right."

"It's not so bad," Andy said. "Most of the way up, we'll barely have to use our hands. It's only the last twenty feet or so that it gets steep."

"Those are the twenty feet that scare me," Pat said.

By this time, Andy had slipped the rope through the device cinched to his belt, just as he had learned at the rock-climbing gym back home. "Don't be afraid," he said. "This may be our only chance to do some real climbing. The walls in the gym are steeper, and we climb them, don't we?"

Pat shrugged his shoulders. So did Tierney. A few minutes later the three of them were roped together. Andy scrambled up the base of the cliff, followed by his friends.

"Ian, you get on the end of the rope, just like they taught you back in the gym," Andy said.

"I remember what they taught me," Ian said. "They taught me never to climb without an adult."

"I'm practically an adult," Andy said. "And I'm in charge, and I say…"

But it was too late. Ian had already trotted up the path, leaving the three climbers behind.

"Andy, shouldn't we follow him?" Tierney asked.

"Ah, let the baby go," Andy said. "He'll be the one to get in trouble for leaving the group, not us."

7

Twenty minutes later, Andy had changed his mind. They were the ones in trouble. As he had predicted, most of the climb had been easy. The last few feet, though, were much steeper than they had looked from below.

"I see a root," Andy called down to his friends. "If I can reach it, I'll be able to pull us all up."

"Wait, Andy—" Pat began, as he strained to get a better grip. Andy didn't hear him. His attention was focused on the root.

Andy's hands darted up, and his feet scrambled up the side of the cliff wall. Pebbles and dirt rolled down the side of the cliff as Andy shot up the rocky surface. His fingers reached for the root.... And grabbed hold!

Suddenly, Andy heard a cry and felt a mighty tug on his rope. He wrapped both hands around the root, holding on with all of his strength.

Andy looked down. Tierney barely hung onto the wall with one hand and a foot. Dangling below her, Pat swung on the end of the rope, whimpering in fear.

"I...lost...my...grip...." Pat whimpered, his feet kicking wildly.

"Just take it easy!" Andy said, as he hung onto the root with all his might. "We'll...be...all right...."

Andy wondered how long he could hold on. He was about to cry for help at the top of his lungs, when he felt himself lurch downward. Dirt stung his eyes. Blinking, Andy looked up.

The tree root was pulling out of the cliff wall! Soon, it would give way completely, leaving nothing but air between them and the sharp rocks a hundred feet below.

DISCUSSION QUESTIONS

1. *Why did Andy decide to try climbing the wall?*

2. *Is Andy glad to have Ian come on their hike? Explain.*

3. *Would you call Pat and Tierney leaders or followers? Give reasons for your answer.*

4. *Predict what you think will happen next in this story. Talk about the possible endings for it.*

Now compare your predictions with the story.

Pat let out a scream as the root tore from the wall. Andy braced himself, expecting to drop through space, when his downward motion jerked to a stop.

The root was holding! But for how long?

"Just hold on!" Andy said. He knew that holding on was not enough, not if the root was going to give way. If only he had something else to grab onto, he could pull them all to safety.

Something hard clunked on Andy's head.

"Grab on!" commanded a voice. Andy looked up. His father's face peered out from above the edge of the cliff. A thick rope hung from the cliff past Andy's side. He reached out and grabbed it, a split second before the root ripped from the wall and tumbled onto the rocks far below.

Two minutes later, Andy, Pat, and Tierney were flopped on the ground atop the cliff, panting with exhaustion and relief. Andy's mom and dad glared at their son, while Ian stood by with a smug smile on his face.

"It's a good thing Ian hurried back to camp," Andy's dad said. "If he hadn't told me where you were, you'd all be lying in that canyon with broken bones—or worse!"

"One Minute to Midnight"

BUILDING BACKGROUND

Tell students this story gives a twist on the classic haunted house story. Discuss the elements you find in haunted house stories, such as dark nights, creaking stairs, and strange sounds in the darkness.

READING STRATEGY FOCUS: CAUSE AND EFFECT

Remind students that a cause is something that makes something happen. An effect is what happens. To find an effect, ask "What happened?" Ask students to think about what happens in the story to make DeNyce change her mind about having a birthday the day after Halloween.

After Reading

TALK ABOUT IT

Ask students what they would have done if they were DeNyce and all their friends were inside the scary house.

WRITE ABOUT IT

Point out that this story is like many haunted house movies. Discuss how filmmakers use images to build suspense, while writers must rely on words. Tell students that filmmakers carefully plan their movies by using storyboards. A storyboard is like a detailed comic strip, showing every shot in the movie. The sounds an audience would hear are written below each drawing.

Have students pretend that they are filmmakers doing the movie version of "One Minute to Midnight." Have them make storyboards of one of the scenes in the movie. For instance, they could plan out the scene in which DeNyce walks through the old house and hears giggling from upstairs. Have students make a drawing for each moment in the scene. What images and sounds would best convey the mood of the scene?

VOCABULARY

Here are words your students will encounter in this story, along with their appropriate meanings:

blood-curdling—*terrifying*

crept—*moved sneakily*

eerie—*strange and frightening*

mysterious—*unexplained*

pasta—*noodles*

sarcasm—*a mocking way*

shivering—*shaking with cold or fear*

"One Minute to Midnight"

○ ○ ○ ○ ○ ○ ○ ○ ○ ○ ○

The floor creaked under DeNyce's feet as she crept through the dark old house.

○ ○ ○ ○ ○ ○ ○ ○ ○ ○ ○

Halloween was not DeNyce's favorite holiday.

Oh, sure, when she was a little kid, DeNyce had liked dressing up in a costume and going trick or treating. But now she was getting a little old for all of that. In fact, the day after Halloween, DeNyce would turn 13.

DeNyce would never admit it, but she had one other big reason for not liking Halloween. When your birthday falls on November 1, no one ever makes a big deal out of it. It's hard to feel special when you've never had a birthday party. Or when no one wants to share your birthday cake because they're stuffed with Halloween candy.

At school on October 31, all DeNyce's friends could talk about was her friend Charlene's Halloween sleep-over later that night.

"This party is going to rock," said Charlene, as she ate lunch with DeNyce and their two other best buds, Kara and Nancy. "Dad is going all out this year. He's even setting up a spooky haunted house in the attic. You know — the kind where you stick your hands in a bowl of spaghetti and they say it's really worms."

"Dipping your hand into pasta? How exciting," DeNyce said.

"After the haunted house," Charlene continued, ignoring DeNyce's sarcasm, "Dad is putting a tent in the backyard. Since it's Friday, we can stay up all night outside, telling ghost stories."

"Hello?" DeNyce said. "You call that fun? Why sleep on the cold, hard ground in a sleeping bag, when you've got a soft, warm bed indoors?"

The rest of the day dragged on. By the time school was over, DeNyce had decided not to go to Charlene's party. But, as she sat in her room doing math homework, watching leaves fall past her window, DeNyce changed her mind. Even if her heart wasn't in it, she knew her friends would be disappointed if she didn't go.

As it turned out, the party wasn't nearly as good as the girls had hoped. The haunted house Charlene's dad had set up in the attic was dumb, not scary. The horror movie they watched on DVD wouldn't have frightened a baby. Even the food wasn't very good.

It was almost midnight when DeNyce and the others settled down in the tent pitched in Charlene's backyard.

"So," Kara said, "anyone know any good ghost stories?"

No one said a thing.

"I guess maybe we're getting old for this sort of thing," Charlene said. The other girls nodded their heads. They looked bored and a little sad. DeNyce hated to see her friends looking that way.

"Why don't you tell us about the old, empty house next door, Charlene?" DeNyce said. DeNyce looked at her friends. "One night last summer, Charlene and I saw mysterious lights in the house, even though no one has lived there for years...."

"That? That was nothing," Charlene said. "My dad went over there the next day. Kids across the street had snuck in to play cards."

"That's not very scary," Kara said. The other girls agreed. They sat in the tent, staring at each other.

"I'm going to brush my teeth," Charlene said. She got up and left the tent. Kara and Nancy settled into their sleeping bags. As they were about to shut their eyes, they heard Charlene yelling in the yard. The three friends struggled out of their sleeping bags and crawled from the tent. Charlene stood near the hedge, looking at the dark house next door.

"My cat, Sheba, just ran into the old house!" Charlene said. "She goes over there all the time."

"Tell your dad," DeNyce said. "He'll go get her."

"I can't," Charlene whined. "If he knows she went over there again, he'll make me get rid of her. I'm going to go get her myself."

"We'll come with you," Kara said.

"No, just stay here," Charlene said. "If dad looks out, he should see a bunch of us in the tent. I'll be back in five minutes."

DeNyce and the other watched as Charlene snuck into the yard next door and tiptoed up to the back door of the big, old dark house. They watched her open the creaky door and slip into the house.

"I'm cold," Kara said. "Let's get back into the tent."

DeNyce nodded her head in agreement. She was shivering, but it wasn't because of the cold.

The three girls sat in silence for awhile.

"So, what's the story with that house?" Nancy asked.

"They say someone was murdered there years and years ago," Kara said. "They say the ghost of the person who was killed haunts the house."

"That's just a story," DeNyce said. "I went to the library and looked through old newspapers after we saw the lights there. No one was ever murdered in the house."

"That's not what I hear," Kara said. The girls sat in silence some more.

"How long has she been gone?" Nancy finally asked.

DeNyce checked her watch. "Almost ten minutes," she said. "That's it!" Kara said, crawling out of her sleeping bag. "I'm going to go find her."

"Should we come with you?" Nancy asked.

Kara shook her head. "Sit tight. If Charlene's dad comes out, tell him we went for a walk." Kara slipped out of the tent and into the night.

DeNyce was really shivering now. She sat opposite Nancy. Neither of them were smiling.

"Do you believe in ghosts?" DeNyce asked.

"Of course not," Nancy said. "Why? Do you?"

DeNyce forced a laugh. "Do I look like a little kid?"

The two girls sat quietly for a while.

"What time is it?" Nancy finally asked.

"Almost midnight," DeNyce said. "Kara has been gone for ten minutes."

Nancy sighed and pushed her way out of her sleeping bag. "I'm going to find them," Nancy told DeNyce.

"No!" DeNyce said. "Shouldn't we wait here?"

"Don't worry," Nancy said. "It's a big house. Maybe they got lost in there. We'll be back before you know it."

Nancy crawled out of the tent, leaving DeNyce alone.

DeNyce curled up in her sleeping bag, telling herself over and over that there were no such things as ghosts. So, what was going on next door? Her friends were split up in the dark house, looking for Charlene's missing cat. Yes, that must be it. They would all be back soon.

DeNyce looked at her watch. It was one minute to midnight. DeNyce gulped. Charlene had been gone for almost a half hour!

SHRIEEEEEEEEK! DeNyce nearly jumped out of her skin at hearing a loud, blood-curdling scream!

STOP HERE

DISCUSSION QUESTIONS

1. *How does DeNyce feel about Halloween? Why?*

2. *Does DeNyce look forward to Charlene's party? How do you know?*

3. *What happens at the party?*

4. *Why does Charlene go to the house next door? Who follows her over there? Why? Predict what you think will happen next in this story.*

Now continue reading to see if you were right.

"Guys? Are you in here?" The floor creaked under DeNyce's feet as she crept through the dark old house. After hearing the scream, DeNyce had gone into Charlene's house, looking for her dad. He wasn't there! So DeNyce decided to go and find her friends for herself.

The old house was cold. As she entered the living room, DeNyce could feel a draft. Then she heard an eerie sound... it sounded like someone giggling. The strange laughter was coming from up the stairs.

DeNyce gathered her courage and walked up the steps. At the top of the stairs, she saw light glowing from under a closed door.

"Guys?" DeNyce asked. "Are you in there?" There was dead silence.

"Okay, guys, this isn't funny," DeNyce said. She walked up to the door. "I'm coming in now. Okay?"

DeNyce put her hand on the door knob. She closed her eyes, bit her lip, and threw open the door—

"SURPRISE!" Charlene, Kara, and Nancy stood at a table. Charlene's dad was with them. Birthday gifts and a birthday cake were on the table.

DeNyce staggered back as the girls, laughing, sang "Happy birthday."

Later, as the girls settled down for the night, Charlene smiled at DeNyce.

The girls laughed. "Sorry to scare you," Nancy said. "But that's the fun of having a birthday the day after Halloween. You can get scared on Halloween, and have a cool birthday, too!"

DeNyce smiled as she curled up in her sleeping bag. "You're right," DeNyce said. "But only if you have cool friends!"

"The Runaway Monster"

Before Reading

BUILDING BACKGROUND

This story is set in an amusement park. Take a poll of students to see how many have visited an amusement park. Ask students if they have dared to get on a roller coaster or any other hair-raising ride. Let students who have ridden a roller coaster describe the experience.

READING STRATEGY FOCUS: MAKING INFERENCES

An inference is a reasonable guess based on text clues as well as the reader's own knowledge and experience. Ask students to make an inference about Martin's motives in this story.

After Reading

TALK ABOUT IT

Revisit your "Building Background" conversation. Have students brainstorm the most exciting parts of their favorite amusement park rides (such as corkscrew twists, steep drops, banked curves). List student responses. Then let students design and draw their versions of "The Runaway Monster," using their responses as a resource.

WRITE ABOUT IT

Have students use their drawings to write about the most terrifying ride imaginable.

VOCABULARY

Here are words your students will encounter in this story, along with their appropriate meanings:

achievement—piece of work, accomplishment

attendant—person taking care of riders

babbling—senseless talk

determination—what you have when your mind is made up

grinding—harsh-sounding

panicked—very frightened

plunged—fell, dropped

scolded—said with anger

sheepishly—bashfully, shyly

snaking—winding

squeaky—high-pitched

staggered—walked clumsily, stumbled

"The Runaway Monster"

○ ○ ○ ○ ○ ○ ○ ○ ○ ○ ○

Just how scary is the "Monster"?
Karen and Ashley are about to find out!

○ ○ ○ ○ ○ ○ ○ ○ ○ ○ ○

The "Monster" was the hottest ride at the Sugar Loaf Amusement Park. In the two weeks since it had opened, thousands of people had taken a ride on the huge, twisting roller coaster. What made the Monster so special? It was the first indoor roller coaster. Riders rode the Monster in pitch darkness!

A great roller coaster that traveled in the dark? It was too good to be true for roller coaster fans. They came from all over the country to ride the Monster.

As Ashley and her friend Karen approached the line snaking toward the ride, they saw a sign that read:

YOU ARE 120 MINUTES FROM RIDING THE MONSTER.

"Aw, come on, Ashley," Karen said. "Let's blow this off. We could hit at least five different rides in the next two hours."

Ashley shook her head with determination.

"Eddie Blake rode this Monster," she said. "He bragged about it all week at school. If he can do it, so can I."

"This had better be good," Karen muttered.

"It depends on what you mean by 'good,'" said a squeaky voice. "This is actually a very dangerous ride."

Ashley and Karen turned. A skinny little boy with thick glasses stood behind them in line.

"Oh, yeah?" Ashley asked. "Who made you an expert?"

"I'm not an expert," the boy said, "but my father is. He sells insurance."

"So?" Karen asked.

"It's his job to figure out how dangerous any situation is. My dad said he wouldn't ride on the Monster, not if you paid him. By the way, my name is Martin. May I ride with you two?"

"Why not?" Ashley said with a shrug.

It didn't take long for Ashley to regret allowing Martin to tag along. He knew all of the details of every amusement park accident that ever happened. And he was eager to tell all about them.

"...And then there was the time when the Twister broke down," Martin said. "Twenty-five people were stuck hanging upside-down for five hours. Of course, they were lucky. They could have been victims of the Upsy-Daisy disaster back in '83—"

"Please, Martin!" Ashley said. "That's enough! I mean, it's fascinating to hear about amusement park accidents. But maybe you can tell me all about them later."

"Maybe I could," Martin said. "If we survive this ride."

By this time, Martin and the girls were standing near the entrance of the Monster. From within its dark shadows came the sounds of grinding machinery and the screams of terrified people.

"I think maybe I'll take a pass on this," Karen said, gulping back her fear as she stared wide-eyed at the ride.

"Oh, no you don't," Ashley said, grabbing her friend's shoulder. "I'm not riding this Monster alone."

By this time, they were able to see where the cars for the Monster were loaded. As each car returned to the platform carrying passengers, a few of the people laughed with joy. Most of them, though, looked terrified.

"See the chains that haul the cars up the hill?" Martin said. "If one tiny link snaps, then the car will roll out of control. The passengers would be smashed to bits. Or maybe they'd crash into another car."

"Will you be quiet?" Ashley nearly shouted at Martin. He glanced at her sheepishly, then kept staring at the chain. Ashley heard Martin muttering something to himself.

Soon, the two girls and Martin were ready to board the ride. As they stepped up to their car, Ashley could make out what Martin was muttering.

"We're going to die," he said, over and over again. "We're going to die. We're going to die."

"Martin, stop saying that!" Ashley scolded, as the ride attendant slammed the safety bar down.

"But we're going to die!" Martin whined. "The chain is going to snap! Did you see it? It's all rusted! We're going to die!"

"Martin!"

The ride lurched forward. The car entered the cool darkness, climbing higher, higher. As the car slowly climbed the hill that carried them into the dark building, Martin's terrified babbling grew even louder.

"Martin, be quiet!" Ashley snapped. She felt her heart jump as the car slowly went over the crest of the hill.

"But the chain is going to break!" Martin screamed. "We're going to—"

Crunch!

A harsh grating sound drowned out Martin. The car came to a dead stop. Ashley could hear her own heart beat in the sudden silence.

"What's wrong?" Karen asked, her voice panicked. "Why did we stop?"

"I'm sure it's all right," Ashley said, putting on her bravest voice. "It's probably just some minor problem—"

SNAP!

Ashley screamed as the sharp crack of metal breaking echoed off the walls.

Her scream grew even louder, as the car plunged straight down into the darkness.

The Monster was out of control!

DISCUSSION QUESTIONS

1. *Why is Ashley determined to ride the Monster?*

2. *Why do you think Martin wants to ride the Monster?*

3. *How does Martin's talking about amusement park accidents make Ashley feel? How would you feel if you were Ashley?*

4. *Predict what you think will happen next in this story. Talk about the possible endings for it.*

Now continue reading to compare your predictions with the story.

Ashley shut her eyes and held on for dear life. The Monster pitched her up and down and left and right. She braced herself, expecting to crash into the walls or onto the floor.

Then, after 90 seconds of terror, Ashley felt herself slowing down. She opened one eye. The car she was riding was pulling up to the platform. Another group of riders was waiting to get on.

"That was great!" Karen gushed as they staggered from the ride. Martin was grinning broadly as he helped Ashley get her balance.

"But, I thought the chain broke!" she gasped. "I thought we were doomed!"

"No, that's just a sound effect they added to the ride," Martin said.

"How do you know so much about it?" Karen asked.

Martin blushed. "The fact is, I told you a little white lie before. My dad doesn't sell insurance. He designs amusement park rides. And the Monster is his greatest achievement! Want to ride it again?"

"No thanks!" Ashley said.

"Okay," Martin said. He trotted back to the end of the line.

About four hours later, Ashley and Karen passed by the line of people waiting to ride the Monster. Martin was there. Ashley heard him talking to the two kids ahead of him in line:

"My dad sells insurance," Martin was saying. "He wouldn't ride this ride, not if you paid him. Do you mind if I ride with you?...."

"Attack of the Killer Ninjas"

Before Reading

BUILDING BACKGROUND

Students go behind the scenes on a movie set in this story. The hero, Kip, is a laid-back surfer working as a stuntman on a martial arts movie.

Ask students if any of them has seen a movie starring martial arts heroes like Jackie Chan or Jet Li. Have a fan describe what a "ninja" is for the rest of the class. (Ninjas are masked Japanese warriors who are experts in hand-to-hand combat.)

READING STRATEGY FOCUS: UNDERSTANDING LITERARY ELEMENTS—SETTING

The setting of a story is the time and place in which it happens. The setting can affect what happens and what characters do in a story. Ask students to think about the setting for this story. How does it affect what happens?

After Reading

TALK ABOUT IT

Kip, the "surfer dude" hero of this story, uses a lot of slang in his speech. Have students reread the story, noting slang Kip uses. ("Tasty." "Dude." "Munching." "Sweet." "Whoa." "Heavy duty." "Living large." etc.) Challenge students to come up with their own slang words to express the thoughts Kip shares with his slang.

WRITE ABOUT IT

Have students write a paragraph retelling the story in first person, using Kip's voice. Encourage students to use slang creatively.

VOCABULARY

Here are words your students will encounter in this story, along with their appropriate meanings:

bodyguards—protectors

crouched—squatted down

hurled—threw

lunged—made a swift move

rehearse—practice

respectful—showing that you admire someone

threatening—promising to hurt someone

"Attack of the Killer Ninjas"

○ ○ ○ ○ ○ ○ ○ ○ ○ ○ ○ ○

Kip gets more than he bargained for when he takes a job as a stunt double on a movie set.

○ ○ ○ ○ ○ ○ ○ ○ ○ ○ ○ ○

"This is one tasty job," Kip told himself. He stood off to one side, watching actors rehearse a scene. Dozens of other people ran around, busy fixing lights and setting up a movie camera.

Kip was on the set of a new movie, "Attack of the Killer Ninjas." The movie starred Mickey Chang, the great Chinese movie star. Chang was playing a secret agent sent to protect a movie star from Ninjas. His co-star was Earl Johnson, who played a laid-back surfer dude who becomes Chang's sidekick.

Although Kip had long blond hair and deep tan, he wasn't an actor playing a surfer dude. Kip really was an expert surfer. He had been hired as Earl Johnson's stunt double. When movie fans saw Earl's character ride the waves, they'd really be watching Kip.

The thing is, there weren't many surfing scenes in the movie. That meant Kip spent most of his time hanging out on the set, watching the actors and eating free food. And that's why he thought it was a tasty job.

"Hey, Kip, better lay off those donuts, or you'll be too stuffed to surf!"

Kip laughed as Mickey Chang, the movie's star, jabbed him in the belly.

"You are correct, dude," Kip said. "If you all gave me something to do, I'd stop munching and get to work."

"Tell you what," Chang said, "we need extras for the big fight scene." Kip knew that "extras" was the word used to describe actors who didn't have speaking roles. "You can be one of the guys that the Ninjas beat up."

"Sounds sweet," Kip said. "What do I have to do?"

A nervous-looking man who had overheard the conversation turned on Kip. "Oh, no you don't!" he said. It was Myles Finch, the movie's director. "We need you safe and sound for the surfing scenes," Finch said. "You're not going to be in any of the fight scenes."

Finch turned to Chang. "Have you gotten any more threatening letters?" he asked the movie star.

"Just the one. Don't worry about me," Chang said. "I can take care of myself."

"See that you do," Finch said. With that, Finch moved away to tell his crew how to set up some lights.

"He worries too much," Chang said.

"What letter was he talking about?" Kip asked. Chang took a piece of paper from his pocket and showed it to Kip. It contained a message spelled out with letters cut from newspapers and magazines:

WATCH YOUR BACK, CHANG! WE WILL GET YOU.

It was signed:

THE REAL NINJAS

"Whoa," Kip said. "That's heavy duty."

Chang shrugged his shoulders. "Everyone in show business gets letters from weirdos. So, do you still want to be in the fight scene?"

"Oh, yeah," Kip said.

"Good," Chang said. "I'll teach you what you need to know. Come to my dressing room at four o'clock. That's when I'm going to rehearse the fight with the other extras. I'll show you some karate moves, too."

"Excellent!" Kip said. "I'm there, dude."

The job kept getting sweeter and sweeter. Kip could not believe he was getting paid to surf, eat donuts…and learn karate from Mickey Chang!

It was about a quarter to four as Kip walked up to Chang's trailer. Like most movie stars, Mickey Chang had a large mobile-home trailer all to himself to use as a dressing room.

"This dude is living large," Kip told himself as he knocked on the trailer's door.

There was no answer. So Kip knocked even louder.

"Yo! Mr. Chang!" Kip called out. "I'm here to learn!"

Kip heard footsteps. He turned around. Three men, all dressed in black, stepped around the corner of the trailer. They stopped and stared at Kip.

"Hey, dudes," Kip said with a friendly nod. "Are you buddies of Mr. Chang, or what?"

The man in the lead of the group snarled at Kip. He turned to his friends and yelled something in a foreign language. The men spread out.

"What's up?" Kip asked. "Don't you guys speak English?" The men crouched low as they circled around Kip.

Suddenly, Kip had a thought.

"I get it," he said. "You guys are the extras who are going to be in the scene with me. You're here for the lessons, too."

Kip walked away from the trailer. The three men eyed him. Kip gave a howl and crouched into a karate position, just like he'd seen in a hundred movies.

"Okay, dudes, let's get it on!" Kip yelled. He lunged for the first man. The man grabbed Kip's arm, stepped aside, and give a flip.

Thud!

Kip landed flat on his back.

"Whew. That was swift." Kip rolled over onto his belly and struggled to his feet. "Go slower next time," he told the man. "Let's break it down into parts—"

Thwack!

One of the other men gave a sweeping kick, knocking Kip's feet out from under him. He landed hard on his butt.

"Ouch!" Kip yelped. "Time out! That hurt, dude." The three men stepped up to Kip. One of them pulled Kip to his feet.

"Maybe we should wait for Mr. Chang before we go on with this lesson," Kip said, rubbing his backside. He heard footsteps. Kip turned and saw two men approach the trailer.

"Who are you?" Kip asked the newcomers.

"We're the extras for the fight scene," one of the men said. "Mr. Chang asked us to show up at four to rehearse. Who are you?"

"I'm here to rehearse, too," Kip said. He turned a wary eye on the three men surrounding him. The lead man snarled in Kip's face as he tightened his grip on Kip's collar.

"Hold on," Kip said. "If I'm here to rehearse, and you're here to rehearse, then these dudes are here to—"

The man hurled Kip to the ground.

"Holy cow!" Kip said. "They're the real Ninjas!"

The three men jumped on Kip.

STOP HERE

DISCUSSION QUESTIONS

1. *What is Kip's job on the movie set? Why does he accept Chang's offer to learn karate?*

2. *Who does Kip meet outside Chang's trailer?*

3. *At first, what does Kip think the men are there for? What does he think at the end of page 23?*

4. *Predict what you think will happen next in this story. Talk about the possible endings for it.*

Now continue reading to compare your predictions with the story.

"Stop!"

Mickey Chang's voice echoed through the air. The three "Ninjas" looked up from Kip. Chang stood in the distance. He said something in Chinese to the three men. They immediately let Kip go and stepped back from him.

Kip got to his feet as Chang walked up.

"Kip, I hope you're not hurt," the star said.

"Nothing that won't heal," Kip said, rubbing his sore head. "What's up with these Ninjas? If they're out to get you, why do they follow orders?"

Chang gave a laugh. "These aren't Ninjas!" he said. "This is my cousin, Han, and two of his friends." The three men each gave Kip a respectful bow. "I hired them as my bodyguards," Chang explained. "They must have thought you were here to hurt me."

"Ah," Kip muttered. "Well, I think I'll go now."

"What's wrong?" Chang asked as Kip limped away. "Don't you want your karate lesson?"

"I already had one," Kip said with a pained smile. "I learned enough to know that my place is on a surfboard!"

"The Mystery in the Backyard"

Before Reading

BUILDING BACKGROUND

Tell students that this is a mystery story. Ask students about the elements often found in mystery stories. List them on the chalkboard. A mystery contains:

- a crime to be solved.
- a criminal to be caught.
- a detective to solve the crime and capture the criminal.

As they read, students should try to identify the story's detective, criminal, and crime. But make sure students understand that a good mystery always contains a few surprises.

READING STRATEGY FOCUS: READING FOR DETAILS

Paying attention to details in a story can help a reader understand ideas and answer questions. In a mystery story, paying attention to details can help solve the mystery.

VOCABULARY

Here are words your students will encounter in this story, along with their appropriate meanings:

brochures—pamphlets on nice paper, usually ads

chanted—said in a sing-song voice

distracted—not able to concentrate

grouch—mean person

inspiration—a great idea

previous—having come before

sarcastic—not serious

suspicious—distrustful

whining—complaining in an annoying way

After Reading

TALK ABOUT IT

Return to your discussion of mystery stories. Tell students that in a typical mystery, the detective gathers clues in order to solve the mystery. Working as a group, list the clues uncovered by Tony and Juan in the story (Mr. Kaufman's missing mother, the new computer, the travel brochures, the "guide to murder" book, the bones buried in the garden).

Let a volunteer describe Tony's theory of what the clues added up to. Have another volunteer describe what the clues actually meant.

WRITE ABOUT IT

Brainstorm with the class another possible theory to explain the various clues presented in the story. Let students write their own ending to the story, in which the clues add up to a different solution to the mystery than either Tony's theory or what actually happened in the story.

"The Mystery in the Backyard"

Tony saw what he held, then yelped with fear and dropped it... It was a bone!

"You kids keep out of my yard!"

Tony and Juan looked up. Old man Kaufman stood on his back porch, shaking his fist at the two boys. Juan forced a friendly smile.

"Sorry, Mr. Kaufman," Juan said. "We tossed our ball over your fence by accident. I think it landed in your garden."

"I said go!" Mr. Kaufman yelled, his face red with anger. Kaufman grabbed a broom from the porch and started to run after the boys. Tony and Juan sprinted back to the fence, and jumped over it to the safety of the alley.

"What a grouch!" Juan panted, as he and Tony stopped to catch their breath.

"Tell me about it," Tony said. "You're lucky to live two blocks away. I have to put up with Kaufman as a neighbor."

"So?" Juan replied. "I'm the one who lost a baseball! What am I going to tell my dad when he asks where it is?"

Clunk!

Something had sailed over the fence and landed smack on Juan's head. He picked it up. It was his baseball. Old man Kaufman had tossed it out of his yard.

"Thank you, Mr. Kaufman!" The boys chanted, sarcastically.

"And stay out!" the old man yelled from behind the fence.

At dinner that night, Tony was whining about Mr. Kaufman.

"Whenever I walk past his house, he's sitting on the front stoop, staring at me, like he expects me to rob him or something. I never did anything to him!"

"Mr. Kaufman has a hard life," Tony's mother gently explained. "I don't know how he makes ends meet, not since he lost his job as a newspaper reporter."

"Just because he doesn't have a job, that doesn't give him the right to yell at me and my friends," Tony muttered.

Tony's father laid down his newspaper and stared at his son. "No," he said. "By the same token, you don't have the right to judge him. Not unless you know what he's gone through." Tony's father shook his head, then picked his newspaper back up. "Imagine what it must be like, paying rent and feeding yourself and your sick old mother...without a steady job!"

Something his father had said made Tony think.

Tony knew that Mr. Kaufman shared the house with his elderly mother. At nights, as he lay in bed, Tony could hear the old woman's screechy voice as she ordered her son around.

The funny thing was, it had been weeks since Tony had seen or heard her.

Tony decided to keep an eye out for Mr. Kaufman—and his missing mother.

Two days later, Tony sat on his front stoop, reading a book. Mr. Kaufman sat on his stoop, staring at the street and not saying a word. Over the previous days, Tony hadn't seen or heard a sign of Kaufman's mother. Now, it was as if Kaufman were waiting for someone. But who?

A delivery truck pulled up in front of Kaufman's house. Tony buried his nose in his book, all the time listening closely as the delivery man trotted up to greet Mr. Kaufman.

"Sign here, please," he said, handing Kaufman a clipboard. "Where do you want it?"

"In here," Kaufman said, shooting suspicious looks up and down the street. He led the delivery man into his house. Tony stole a glance at the delivery—three large cardboard boxes.

Later that night, Tony glanced out the window of his family's bathroom. From there, he could see across the yard and through a window into Kaufman's house. What he saw surprised him. Kaufman stood alongside three empty cardboard boxes, reading a thick owner's manual. On a desk, he had set up a brand new computer with a big, sturdy printer.

Tony gasped.

"If he's so poor, how can he afford a new computer?" Tony asked himself.

Early the next morning, Tony's mom pulled a full bag out of the trash can.

"I'll take the garbage out, Mom," Tony said, rushing up to take the bag from her. She looked at him, shocked.

"What's gotten into him?" she asked her husband as Tony headed down the back stairs.

Once he was in the alley, Tony dropped the garbage bag into a trash can. Looking around to make sure the coast was clear, he headed to the garbage cans and stacks of newspapers outside Kaufman's fence.

Tony gasped. Leaning against the fence were stacks of freshly bundled glossy brochures. Tony looked at them. They were advertisements for fancy cruises, resorts on tropical islands, and other costly vacations.

"If he's so poor, why is he shopping for an expensive trip?" Tony asked himself.

The next day, Tony told Juan about his discoveries.

"It's just like this old movie I saw," Tony said. "I'll bet he killed the old lady!"

"I don't know," Juan said. "Why would he do that?"

"So he could get all of her money, of course," Tony said. "He killed her and took her fortune. Now he's just waiting for a chance to get away." Tony had a sudden thought and snapped his fingers. "I'll bet that's why he chased us away from his garden. That's where he buried her body!"

Juan groaned. "I think you're nuts."

"Oh, yeah?" Tony replied. "If he didn't kill her, then where is she? No one has seen her for weeks. And how was he able to afford a new computer? And why was he looking at ads for expensive trips?"

"There could be a million reasons for any of those things," Juan said.

"Maybe," Tony admitted. "But all together, they add up to murder."

Juan shook his head. "I don't think so," he said.

Tony decided to challenge his friend. "All right. Join me in some detective work. We'll follow old man Kaufman around. If we see his mother, or learn how he's making his money, then I'll eat my words. If not, we'll tip off the cops."

Tony held out his hand. Juan hesitated a moment, then shook Tony's hand.

It turned out that Mr. Kaufman was pretty easy to follow. Over the next few days, he only made a few trips to the corner store to buy some groceries. On Friday he went to the post office to mail some bills. That night he went to a church hall to play some bingo.

Juan and Tony followed him every step of the way. Although Mr. Kaufman didn't do anything suspicious, the two boys didn't see a sign of his mother. She'd been missing for weeks now. Tony was more certain than ever that she had been the victim of foul play.

On Saturday, the boys got a break. Kaufman left his house in the

28

middle of the morning and shuffled off to the public library. Tony and Juan followed. They hung out in the kids' section, watching as Kaufman gathered a large stack of books from the shelves. He sat at a table, carefully going through the books and making notes of information he found in them. After four hours of work, Kaufman stood and stretched, then headed out the door.

Juan moved to follow him.

"Wait!" Tony hissed. He led Juan over to the table where Kaufman had been working. Tony looked at the titles of the books Kaufman had been reading. He gasped at what he saw:

> *True Crime*
> *Murder and Mayhem*
> *The Writer's Guide to Getting Away With Murder*

"Now what do you say?" Tony asked, staring at Juan with eyes wide.

Juan gulped. "I say we should find out exactly what Kaufman has planted in his garden," Juan said.

It was dark and cloudy when the boys scrambled over the fence into Kaufman's yard late that night. His windows were black. The only sound was the distant rumble of traffic on the avenue.

"This way," Tony whispered. He led Juan to the garden.

Each boy carried a stick. As they had planned, Juan and Tony started at opposite ends of the garden, jabbing their sticks into the earth. After a few minutes of poking around, Tony's stick hit something hard about ten inches beneath the surface.

"I found something!" he hissed. Juan came to his side as Tony began to dig.

"What is it?" Juan asked.

"Sssssh." Tony pulled something long and hard from the dirt.

The moon appeared from behind a cloud. A shaft of pale light fell on the yard. Tony saw what he held, then yelped with fear and dropped it.

It was a bone!

"Who's out there?" yelled a harsh voice. It was Kaufman!

"Run!" Tony hissed.

Too late. A beam of light from a flashlight knifed from Kaufman's porch across the yard, landing on Tony's blinking face.

STOP HERE

DISCUSSION QUESTIONS

1. *In the beginning of the story, how does Mr. Kaufman treat Tony and Juan? How do they feel about him?*

2. *What does Tony suspect that Mr. Kaufman has done? What clues does he find to support his suspicion?*

3. *Does Juan agree with Tony? What convinces him that Tony may be right about Mr. Kaufman?*

4. *Predict what you think will happen next in this story. Talk about the possible endings for it.*

Now continue reading to compare your predictions with the story.

Tony sat at his kitchen table. He wished he could have been hiding under it. Juan's parents had just left after coming to pick up their son. Now, old man Kaufman sat at the table opposite Tony, sipping a cup of coffee. Tony's parents stood nearby. Although they were acting very nice, Tony knew that as soon as Kaufman left their smiles would disappear.

"I'm sorry if I've been a bad neighbor," Kaufman said. "Privacy is important to me. Writing isn't easy, I don't like to be distracted."

"We understand," Tony's mom said. "And congratulations on selling your first book."

"Thanks," he said. "With the money I've earned, I was able to send my poor mother on a long vacation. Goodness knows she deserved it. And at last I was able to afford a computer."

Tony looked at Mr. Kaufman with suspicion. "What about the bone I found buried in your garden?" he asked.

"Promise you won't tell the police?" Mr. Kaufman asked. "It's against the law to bury your pets in your yard. But when our old dog Poochie died five years ago, it broke mother's heart. We had to keep the old boy nearby."

Tony was still not convinced. "I saw you in the library today," Tony said. "You were reading some interesting stuff."

"I was doing research for my next book," Mr. Kaufman said. "This one will be a murder mystery." He smiled at Tony. "I think I've got an inspiration," Kaufman said. "It's going to star a boy detective!"

Even Tony had to smile as the three adults broke into laughter.

HEX FILE #N246-3
"The Man on the Moon"

FOR THE
TEACHER

Before Reading

BUILDING BACKGROUND

This story looks at science fiction fans who take their favorite shows and characters too seriously.

Discuss with students why these stories are called *science* fiction. Have a volunteer define the word "science." (Science involves a careful study of facts.) Have another volunteer define "fiction." (Fiction refers to imaginary stories.)

Discuss how science fiction is different from straight fantasy stories, such as the "Harry Potter" novels. Students should understand that science fiction stories are imaginary works that feature fantastic elements which are scientifically possible (such as life on other planets), if not yet proven. Fantasy stories feature elements that are scientifically impossible.

READING STRATEGY FOCUS: UNDERSTANDING THE GENRE OF SCIENCE FICTION

Discuss with students common elements of science fiction:

- ○ is often set in the future
- ○ often involves space exploration or time travel
- ○ often features aliens from other planets
- ○ usually tells an adventure story

After Reading

TALK ABOUT IT

Discuss how Andy Roid was caught lying because he did not know facts about the Apollo space program.

WRITE ABOUT IT

Working with students, brainstorm a list of questions they have about the Apollo program. Record the questions on the chalkboard. Have students work in teams to do research at a library or on the Internet to answer the questions.

VOCABULARY

Here are words your students will encounter in this story, along with their appropriate meanings:

antennae—wires sticking out from the head

auditorium—large room with a stage and many seats

astronauts—scientists who travel into space

awed—very impressed

bizarre—strange

convenient—lucky

convention—a large gathering of people

creature—a living being

murmured—spoke in low tones

plaque—a flat plate of engraved metal used as a memorial

recruit—find and hire

scoff—make fun of

stampede—mad rush by a crowd

HEX FILE #N246-3
"The Man on the Moon"

"That's a bizarre costume," the man said, eyeing Muldew's suit and tie. "Who are you guys supposed to be? One of the Men in Black?"

Agent Skilly turned to her partner, Agent Muldew. "If I see one more space alien, I think I'll scream," she said.

The two FBI agents were on a case. They weren't chasing space aliens. They were at a convention for science fiction buffs. All around them people were shopping for rare comic books, movie posters, and other fun stuff. Most of the people wore costumes based on their favorite science fiction characters. There were dozens of people dressed as characters from "Star Yech." Even more people were done up in costumes from the different "Star Chores" movies.

Skilly and Muldew were at the convention looking for a man named Andy Roid. The FBI had gotten a tip that Roid claimed to have been kidnapped by space aliens. Roid was the guest of honor at the convention. Skilly and Muldew were sent to check out his story.

Muldew stopped at a booth where a man was selling tapes of the old TV show, "My Uncle, The Martian." The man wore silver antennae and a suit made of tin foil. He gave Muldew a suspicious look.

"That's a bizarre costume," the man said, eyeing Muldew's suit and tie. "Who are you supposed to be? One of the Men in Black?"

"I'm an FBI agent. I'm here doing my job," Muldew said, flashing his badge. The Man in Tin Foil stood straight and gave Muldew a salute.

"I'm at your service, sir!" he told Muldew. He leaned in and whispered, "If you are here to recruit undercover agents to go aboard alien space ships, then sign me up!"

"Not exactly," Skilly said. "We're here to investigate the story of a man named Andy Roid. Do you know him?"

The Man in Tin Foil got an awed look on his face. "No, I don't. But I wish I did! He has seen things the rest of us can only dream about."

"Where can we see him?" Muldew asked. The man checked his watch.

"Right now," he said. "Roid is giving a lecture in the auditorium. If you hurry, you can catch it."

Muldew and Skilly turned toward the auditorium.

"After the lecture, maybe you'd like to buy one of my tapes," the man said, hopefully holding one up.

"Maybe," Muldew said with a polite smile. He turned to his partner. "A TV show about space aliens living on Earth?" he whispered. "That's the dumbest thing I ever heard."

The auditorium was packed by the time Muldew and Skilly got there. Just about everyone there was dressed in a costume. In fact, out of the hundred or so people crowded in the room, only three were not dressed as space aliens: Skilly, Muldew, and the man of the hour...Andy Roid.

Roid stood on a stage. He wore a plain white sweater and jeans. A drawing of a bald creature with large dark eyes was projected onto a big screen behind him.

"I call the aliens "Grays," because that is the color of their skin," Roid was saying. "Unfortunately, I don't have any photographs of the aliens. When they kidnapped me, I didn't have a camera with me."

"How convenient," Skilly whispered to Muldew.

Roid told about his experience with the "Grays." He said he noticed strange lights in the sky above his house one night. Roid went into his yard to see what was going on. A blinding white light from the sky landed on him. He passed out. When he woke up, Roid was onboard a space ship, surrounded by aliens!

Roid claimed that the space ship had taken him back to the aliens' home planet, which orbited a star called Rigel. After they kept him on their planet for a week, the aliens brought Roid back to Earth.

"You can read all about it if you buy my book," Roid said. "Before I start autographing copies, does anyone have any questions?"

There was a stampede for the microphones. Everyone in the audience had questions for Roid.

"Were you probed by the aliens?" one man asked.

"Not at all," Roid said. "They were very polite. Next question."

"I want to meet an alien!" a woman yelled into the microphone. "I want to visit another planet! Why did they pick you and not me?"

Roid gave a little smile. "You'd have to ask the aliens the answer to that," he said. "Next question."

"What language do the aliens speak?" another person asked.

"None," Roid said. "They read minds. They never have to talk. Next?"

An eager young man took to the microphone. "What was the coolest part of your trip?" he asked. "Was it getting kidnapped in a beam of light? Or hanging out on the aliens' ship? Or visiting another planet?"

Roid got a serious look on his face. "I'll tell you what the best part of the trip was," he said. "On our way back to Earth, the aliens stopped on the far side of the moon. We were right at the spot where the first astronauts landed back in 1969. One of the aliens took me to the plaque those astronauts left. He pointed to the words on it…'We Came in Peace.' The alien nodded and tapped himself on the chest. They, too, had come in peace. Then we stood together and watched the sun rise over the Sea of Tranquillity. That's when I knew the aliens were here to help us, not hurt us."

The room fell silent. The space buffs were in awe of Roid's story. Skilly saw her chance and went to the microphone.

"Do you have a question, young lady?" Roid asked her.

"Yes, I do," Skilly asked. "Why are you lying to these people?"

The crowd turned on Skilly and started to boo.

"How do you know he's not telling the truth?" one man yelled. "Can you prove it?"

"Sure she can!" Muldew yelled back. "And so could you, if you stopped to think."

DISCUSSION QUESTIONS

1. What kind of people were at the science fiction convention? What words could you use to describe them?

2. How is Andy Roid like the other people at the convention? How is he different?

3. Would you trust Roid if you heard his story? Why or why not?

4. Why do Skilly and Muldew know that Roid is a fake? What about his story doesn't add up? Talk about the possible endings for this story.

Now continue reading to see if you were right.

Andy Roid quieted the angry crowd. "There are always people ready to scoff at the truth," he said. "Don't let them shake your trust in me."

"And there are always people ready to rip you off," Skilly told the crowd. "Don't give him money for a book that he says is true, when he really made it all up!"

"How do you know that I made it up?" Roid said.

"Do you stand by your story about visiting the moon?" Muldew asked.

"Of course," Roid said. "It was the most important part of my entire journey."

"And it's the part we can prove is a lie," Skilly said. "You said you visited the spot where the astronauts visited the moon…on the far side of the moon. Everyone knows that the astronauts landed on the near side of the moon."

"Well, yes," Roid sputtered. "It was facing Earth when the astronauts landed there, but then it turned away."

"But the moon always shows one side to Earth. The far side never faces Earth!" Skilly said.

The crowd murmured at this. A few people grumbled and headed for the exit.

"Wait! Stop!" Roid said. "Did I say far side of the moon? I meant near side. I mean—"

"What you really mean is that your book should be labeled for what it is," Muldew said. "Science *fiction!*"

HEX FILE #P860-1
"The Trick Sense"

Before Reading

BUILDING BACKGROUND

Tell students that this story is a parody of the hit movie "The Sixth Sense." Explain that a parody is a story that pokes fun at another story. Then ask a volunteer to describe the story of "The Sixth Sense" in his or her own words.

After students have talked about the movie's characters and plot, ask students how they would expect a parody to poke fun at the movie. After students have made their predictions, begin reading the story.

READING STRATEGY FOCUS: VISUALIZING

Readers form pictures in their minds to help them understand what they are reading. Have students choose one scene from the story to visualize.

VOCABULARY

Here are words your students will encounter in this story, along with their appropriate meanings:

headquarters—the home office

imagination—the ability to make things up

shushed—silenced

squinting—looking through half-closed eyes

squirm—a wriggling motion

stroked—petted

After Reading

TALK ABOUT IT

Ask students how Muldew knew that Kyle was lying when he said that he saw ghosts. (The "ghosts" Kyle had seen used or knew about things that were invented after they had supposedly died.)

Have students brainstorm a list of technologies they use all of the time (computers, MP3 players, DVD players, handheld video games, and so on). Then ask students which of the items on their list were not around when their parents were kids. (Students should check to see if they are correct by asking their parents.)

WRITE ABOUT IT

Lead a class discussion on technologies that might be invented by the time students are adults. Guide the discussion by pointing out that new technologies grow out of existing technologies. Ask: How might computers be improved in twenty years? Cars? Airplanes? Have students write a paragraph describing a technology they'd like to see invented.

HEX FILE #P860-1
"The Trick Sense"

○ ○ ○ ○ ○ ○ ○ ○ ○ ○ ○

Are Skilly and Muldew up to solving this ghostly challenge?

○ ○ ○ ○ ○ ○ ○ ○ ○ ○ ○

The little boy huddled on the sofa. He looked scared and alone. FBI Agents Skilly and Muldew sat in chairs nearby.

"Kyle, you're frightened, aren't you?" Skilly gently asked the boy.

"All of the time," the little boy whispered.

"Will you tell me why are you frightened, Kyle?" Muldew asked.

Kyle shook his head no.

"Pretty please?" Skilly asked. "If you don't tell us what's bothering you, then we can't help you. And that's why we're here."

Kyle looked at Skilly, then Muldew.

"Can you keep a secret?" Kyle asked. Skilly and Muldew nodded. His eyes squinting with fear, the boy leaned in on the FBI agents. "I see dead people," Kyle whispered.

Kyle's mother, watching from the kitchen, gave a sob and turned away. Skilly smiled sadly and stroked the little boy on the head.

Muldew got a confused look on his face. "Wait a second," he said. "Haven't I heard this somewhere before?"

Skilly 'shushed' her partner. "Where do you see dead people?" she asked Kyle.

"There's one right behind you now," Kyle said.

Skilly jumped, startled, and turned around. There was no one there.

Muldew laughed. "Ha! He got you!" Muldew said.

"No, it's true," Kyle said. "There is a ghost there." The little boy blinked back the tears. "No one believes me. I see ghosts no one else can see. It's terrible. Terrible!"

"We believe you," Skilly said. "Tell us more. Do you see ghosts everywhere?"

Kyle shook his head. "Not everywhere, just most places. It's the worst at school. I also see a lot of them at the library. And at the dentist's office."

"Hmmm." Muldew stroked his chin, thoughtful. "Kyle, are there any places where you *don't* see ghosts?"

Kyle's mom came into the room. "He doesn't see the ghosts at newer buildings," she explained. "Kyle is okay at the mall, or the movie theater, or the video arcade."

"I think I see a pattern here," Muldew said.

Kyle's mom stepped up to the boy. "Kyle, I'm going to visit Grandma this afternoon," she said. "Do you want to come along?"

"Aw, gee, I'd love to, Mom," he said. "But the last time we visited Grandma I saw eighteen ghosts. Remember how scared I was?"

"I remember," Kyle's mom said. "It's okay. While I'm at grandma's you can go to the movies."

Kyle forced a brave smile onto his face. "Thanks, Mom," he said.

Muldew and Skilly stepped into another room to talk about the case.

"The poor kid," Skilly said. "He has a bad case of E.S.P. It must be awful."

"You think so?" Muldew said. "I'd say he's doing pretty well for himself."

"What do you mean?" Skilly asked.

"He only sees ghosts in places he doesn't want to go," Muldew said. "It gives him an excuse to skip school or blow off a trip to the dentist. It's like calling in sick. But if you claim to see ghosts, you don't need a note from your doctor."

"So you think he's faking?"

"It wouldn't surprise me," Muldew said.

"Do you think we can prove it?" asked Skilly.

Muldew shrugged his shoulders. "We can try. Let's take him down to headquarters and ask him a few questions."

Two hours later, Kyle sat at a table in the FBI offices. Wires were taped to his head and the palms of his hands. The wires ran to a lie detector machine.

Muldew and Skilly sat across the table from Kyle. "Don't be nervous," Skilly said.

"I'm not," Kyle said. "After you've seen the ghosts I've seen, a couple of FBI ghosts won't scare you."

"You see ghosts here at FBI headquarters?" Muldew asked.

"Sure," Kyle said. "There's one sitting right beside you."

Muldew couldn't help but squirm. Skilly looked at the lie detector. It indicated that Kyle was telling the truth.

"What's the name of the ghost?" Muldew asked, taking out his notebook.

Kyle wrinkled his forehead, as if he was listening to someone. "He says his name is Jones...." Kyle listened some more, then smiled. "He was a very good FBI agent. President Kennedy gave him a medal back in 1960."

Skilly looked at the lie detector. The needle was steady. The machine still showed that Kyle was telling the truth.

Skilly and Muldew asked Kyle all about the other ghosts he had seen.

Kyle described the ghost of Mrs. Dalloway, an old woman who used to live in his mother's house. Mrs. Dalloway had told him what it was like when she was a girl. Her most vivid memory was hearing about the sinking of the *Titanic* on the radio.

Then there was Jackie, the ghost of a little girl in his classroom at school. Jackie had been a real computer whiz back in 1975.

The scariest ghost Kyle saw was a kid named Bungee. Bungee had been an all-star dare-devil at the X-Games throughout the 1980s.

After an hour of asking Kyle questions, Agents Skilly and Muldew left him. They stepped into the next room to talk about the case.

"He's obviously a fake," Muldew said.

"Huh?" Skilly asked. "How do you know that? The lie detector hasn't moved an inch. He isn't lying."

"Well, if he isn't lying, then every ghost he sees has been lying to him!"

"How can you be sure?" Skilly asked.

"Easy!" Muldew said. "It's because—"

> ### DISCUSSION QUESTIONS
>
> 1. *Why does Muldew suspect that Kyle might be lying?*
>
> 2. *How do Muldew and Skilly plan to prove whether or not Kyle is telling the truth?*
>
> 3. *After they question Kyle, does Skilly continue to think that the boy is telling the truth? Why or why not?*
>
> 4. *Why does Muldew think that Kyle is lying? Think about what Kyle told the agents. What about his different stories does not add up? Talk about the possible endings for this story.*

Now continue reading to see if you were right.

Kyle's mom scowled at her son. Kyle stared at his feet.

"So you've been lying all along?" she asked.

"Not exactly," Kyle said. "I was just using my imagination. That's good, right?"

Kyle's mom growled with anger. "Go to your room. We'll talk about this later."

As Kyle trooped off to his room, his mother turned to Agents Skilly and Muldew. "Thank you for clueing me in on what Kyle's been up to," she said. "How did you figure out that he was fibbing?"

"It wasn't easy. Kyle told some very interesting stories about his ghosts," Skilly said. "And he was so convincing that he fooled a lie detector test."

"But he got his facts wrong," Muldew said, as he looked at his notebook. "Kyle said one of the ghosts got a medal from President Kennedy in 1960. Kennedy didn't become President until 1961."

"Kyle also said that another ghost listened to radio reports of the *Titanic* sinking," Skilly said. "But radio wasn't around until ten years after the *Titanic* sank."

"He also claimed one of the ghosts was a little girl from 1975," Muldew added. "Kyle said the little girl was a computer whiz, but no little kid would have worked on a computer in the early 1970s. Personal computers didn't become common until later."

"And Kyle said one of the ghosts was an X-Games star in the 1980s," Skilly said, shaking her head. "The X-Games didn't come along until the 1990s."

"I've got to keep on eye on that boy," Kyle's mom said.

"That's a good idea, ma'am," Muldew said, closing his notebook. "And if he sees any more dead people, make sure they've got their facts straight before you call in the FBI."

HEX FILE #D1304-8
"El Pie Grande"

BUILDING BACKGROUND

In this story, Skilly and Muldew meet a globe-trotting archaeologist. Point out that the characters Lara Croft from "Tomb Raider" and Indiana Jones from the "Raiders of the Lost Ark" movies are archaeologists. Ask students familiar with these characters to describe the sort of adventures they have. Elicit that the characters travel to exotic places in search of ancient artifacts.

Point out to students that archaeology is a respected science dedicated to the study of ancient cultures. Tell students that many of the things they have seen in museums, including mummies, were found and studied by archaeologists.

This story also features a variation on the Bigfoot and Abominable Snowman legends. Ask a student familiar with these legends to describe them in his or her own words.

READING STRATEGY FOCUS: ANALYZING CHARACTER

Have students think about the character of T. Don Looney. Encourage them to pay attention to the things he says and does as they read the story that support their character description.

VOCABULARY

Here are words your students will encounter in this story, along with their appropriate meanings:

appearances—the way things seem on the surface

archaeology—the science studying ancient peoples

billionaire—a very wealthy person

expedition—an organized trip

fierce—wild and dangerous

fortunately—luckily

offended—with hurt feelings

remote—far off, isolated

vowed—said with determination

After Reading

TALK ABOUT IT

Ask students to think of other legends or tall tales they've heard of. Invite them to share some of the stories. Ask them to think about and discuss why people like to tell these kinds of stories.

WRITE ABOUT IT

Present students with a list of archaeological discoveries. Have students pick a discovery to research and write a report on. Possible topics include:

- Machu Picchu
- King Tut's tomb
- Troy
- Pompeii
- Jamestown
- Mesa Verde
- Stonehenge

HEX FILE #D1304-8
"El Pie Grande"

○○○○○○○○○○○○

I heard a terrifying howl. I asked my guide what it was. "El Pie Grande," he said. That's Spanish for "Bigfoot."

○○○○○○○○○○○○

T. Don Looney was one smart guy. Practically overnight, he had gone from poor computer nerd to software billionaire. Yet, as quickly as he had made his fortune, Looney seemed to be in a bigger hurry to spend it.

Despite his brains, Looney had a big heart. He was very honest and believed everyone else was as honest as he was. As a result, just about every shady character in America with a get-rich-quick scheme came to Looney, asking for money.

Fortunately for Looney, his ex-girlfriend was FBI Agent Skilly. If Looney trusted everyone, Skilly was the opposite. It was her job to discover the truth behind appearances. Skilly did her best to protect her old friend Looney from con artists.

"I'm telling you, Dr. Loft is for real," Looney told Skilly. They were driving across the campus of State University. "If she is a con artist, then how did she get a job as a college professor?"

"If she is a con artist, I'll find out," Skilly replied. "That's why you asked me to tag along, right?"

Looney sighed, then nodded.

Skilly and Looney were on their way to visit the famous scientist Dr. Cora Loft. Loft traveled the globe looking for treasures from the ancient world. She had sent a letter to T. Don Looney, inviting him to visit her. She wanted to tell him all about her latest discovery.

To Skilly, that meant one thing. Loft wanted Looney to give her money.

Skilly and Looney walked into the Archaeology Department. It was an old, dusty building. The first person they met there was a gray-haired woman with thick glasses.

"You are Dr. Cora Loft, I presume." Skilly held her hand out to the old woman. "My name is Agent Skilly, and I'm here with—"

"I'm not Cora Loft," the old woman said. "I'm a student." She pointed to another woman. "There's Dr. Cora Loft."

"Now, that's more like it!" T. Don Looney said, a big smile on his face, as he looked at Dr. Cora Loft.

Loft was a pretty young woman wearing shorts and hiking boots, with a big backpack slung over her shoulder. Skilly groaned and shook her head. It was going to be hard to keep Looney from acting like a fool now....

°   °   °

"The legend of *El Pie Grande* goes back thousands of years," Dr. Loft was saying. "Scientists will tell you it is just a myth. I think it's based on the truth."

Skilly and Looney sat in Dr. Loft's office. She was telling them all about her recent trip to South America. Loft had made a great discovery down there. Or so she claimed.

"Many countries have legends like *El Pie Grande*," Loft explained. "In the United States, there is 'Bigfoot,' the giant man-ape who is supposed to live in the mountains out west. In Tibet, they speak of the 'Yeti,' the legendary 'snowman' who lives in the Himalayas. *El Pie Grande* is the South American version of this creature."

Looney gave the beautiful professor a dreamy smile. "That is so fascinating," he said.

"Hmmm," Skilly growled. "It's part of my job to know about strange legends. Why have I never heard of *El Pie Grande* before?"

"Because the legend is told in remote villages in the Andes Mountains," Dr. Loft said. "I first heard about it last year. It was on Christmas Day." Dr. Loft shuddered. "I'll never forget it. I was sleeping in a camp at the base of a mountain when I heard a terrifying howl. I asked my guide what it was. '*El Pie Grande*,' he said. That's Spanish for 'Bigfoot.'"

Dr. Loft opened a diary and looked at her notes there.

"My guide told me that the people in the mountains always hear the howl of *El Pie Grande* at that time of year. According to the legend, the creature leaves the mountain tops at the start of winter and comes to the lower regions to avoid the snow and ice. *El Pie Grande* is supposed to be fierce—no person has ever seen him and lived. Of course, as soon as I heard this, I began my search to find the creature."

Looney gave Dr. Loft an admiring stare. "You are so brave," he said.

"I am a scientist," she said. "I hiked up the mountain in the direction I heard the howl. The rocks were cold and icy. I could see a blizzard raging near the peak of the mountain. I didn't see *El Pie Grande* that day. But I did see this."

Dr. Cora Loft dropped a big slab of plaster on the table. In the center of the plaster was the imprint of a giant naked foot.

T. Don Looney gasped.

"I found this footprint in the snow," Dr. Cora Loft said. "I made a copy of it using plaster of Paris. That's the only evidence of *El Pie Grande* I found. But I'm convinced the creature exists. The legend is real!"

"What do you need to prove it?" Looney asked.

"Just a little money," Dr. Loft said. "I want to mount a full expedition. I can visit the mountain when school is out over Christmas." She got a determined look on her face. "I will find the creature," Dr. Loft vowed.

T. Don Looney whipped out his checkbook. "How much do you need?" he asked.

"Hold on!" Skilly barked. She gave Dr. Loft a cold look. "Before you pay for an expedition to find *El Pie Grande*, I think Dr. Loft should tell you why she really wants the money."

Dr. Loft looked offended. "Are you saying I lied?"

"I'm saying your story doesn't add up," Skilly said. "I know that because—"

DISCUSSION QUESTIONS

1. *Why does Skilly go with her friend T. Don Looney to visit Dr. Loft?*

2. *How does Looney act when he meets Dr. Loft? How does Skilly respond to that?*

3. *What story does Dr. Loft tell Looney? What does she ask him for? Why?*

4. *Why does Skilly think that Dr. Loft is lying? Think about Loft's story. What detail or details about it are not correct? Talk about the possible endings for this story.*

Now continue reading to see if you were right.

Dr. Cora Loft blushed and looked away after Skilly pointed out the obvious: '*El Pie Grande*' wouldn't leave the mountain tops at the start of winter...not in December in South America.

South America is below the equator...where summer starts in December!

"Have you ever even been to South America?" Skilly asked the professor.

"Well...not yet," she admitted. "But with Mr. Looney's financial help I was hoping to go this December." Cora Loft batted her long eyelashes at Looney. "Wouldn't you like to go on an expedition with me?"

T. Don Looney stuffed his checkbook back in his pocket. Without a word, he turned and marched out of the room.

"I didn't even see it coming!" T. Don Looney moaned, as he and Skilly left the building. "If you can't trust a college professor, who can you trust?"

"You can always trust your friendly neighborhood FBI agent," Skilly said with a smile.

HEX FILE #S0058-8
"The Loch Ness Shark"

Before Reading

Ask students if they have heard of the Loch Ness monster. Discuss the legend with students. Point out that "Nessie" is a sea monster that supposedly lives in Loch Ness—a very long, winding, and deep lake in Scotland. Although many people claim to have seen the monster, there have been no clear photos, videos, or other pieces of evidence to prove its existence.

Have students predict what would happen if someone caught the Loch Ness monster on videotape. Elicit that the footage would cause a sensation on television—and could make the person who owns the tape rich.

VOCABULARY

Here are words your students will encounter in this story, along with their appropriate meanings:

commotion—disturbance

huddled—got together for a private talk

scaly—covered with reptile skin

tourists—people on vacation

READING STRATEGY FOCUS: ASKING QUESTIONS

Good readers ask questions as they read to help them understand better. As they read the story, have students write down any questions they have.

After Reading

TALK ABOUT IT

Have students share the questions they had as they read the story. Ask students if their questions were answered by the end of the story.

Then lead a class discussion on Joe Finn's actions and his motives. Get the ball rolling with these questions:

- Why do you think Finn refused to let experts study his tape? (Possible answer: It's a fake.)

- Why did Finn claim that the German tourist Jergens had shot the tape? (Because Finn knew that people would not have trusted the tape had they known that he shot it.)

- Do you think Finn's tape was real? Why or why not? (Possible answer: It was probably false, otherwise he would have let experts study it.)

WRITE ABOUT IT

Use this lesson as the springboard for a discussion on critical viewing skills. Remind students that just because they see something on TV, it's not necessarily true. Whenever they hear a wild claim or see an outrageous image on TV, students should always consider the source and ask themselves if it's reliable. Have students write a paragraph explaining why TV viewers need to consider story sources.

HEX FILE #S0058-8
"The Loch Ness Shark"

Is seeing always believing? In this story,
Skilly and Muldew try to find out.

"Thanks for coming by on such short notice," said Melba Frye as she led Agents Skilly and Muldew down the hall.

"We're just doing our job," said Muldew.

"Me too," said Frye. "It's my job to make sure all of our stories are accurate. I'm not sure about this one."

Skilly and Muldew were paying a visit to the C-NEWS cable television network. Melba Frye worked for one of the network's programs, a popular show called "Amazing But True!" She had called the agents that morning to ask for their help.

"Normally, I can tell if someone is lying," Frye explained as they walked along. "But with a story like this, it's not so easy."

"What's the story?" Muldew asked.

"A man wants to go on the air with proof that the Loch Ness Monster exists," Frye said.

Skilly gave a whistle of surprise. "That's big news...if it's true," she said.

"And that's a big if," Frye said. They stopped outside a meeting room. "My main question—can we trust the man?"

"Why not?" Skilly asked.

Frye threw open the door. Skilly and Muldew saw who was waiting inside. "That's why not!" Muldew groaned.

Sitting at a table was Joe "the Shark" Finn, a well-known criminal. He smiled at the sight of the two FBI agents.

"Yo! If it ain't my old pals Skilly and Muldew!" Finn said. "How's it going?"

"Not bad, Joe," Muldew said. "We haven't seen you since you tried to sell the Washington Monument to Japanese tourists."

"Hey, did I ever thank you for what happened?" Finn asked. "Ever since you guys arrested me, I turned my life around. I'm a new man."

47

"You don't say?" Skilly sounded skeptical. "We hear you have found evidence that the Loch Ness monster is real."

"Not me, my friends! I'm just acting as the agent." Finn pointed to a man sitting across the table from him. The man was big and fat, with short blond hair. "Skilly and Muldew, meet my friend Wolfgang Jergens."

Jergens stood and wrapped Muldew's hand in his own damp, warm paw. As Muldew greeted the man, Jergens said something in a foreign language.

"Hold on," Muldew said. "He's speaking German, right?"

"That is correct," Finn said. "This is his first ever trip to the states. Wolfie doesn't speak a word of English. But with his story, he doesn't have to."

"Give us the details," Skilly said.

"I was over in Scotland for a golf vacation," Finn said. "My hotel was near Loch Ness, the famous lake where a sea monster is supposed to live. One day, when I was heading out to golf, I heard a commotion in the lobby."

Skilly stole a glance at Jergens. The big man was reading a German newspaper, paying no attention to Finn.

"I went into the lobby," Finn continued. "There was Jergens, talking a mile a minute and waving his video camera around. I speak a few words of German, so I was able to understand what he was saying. Jergens had gone for a hike along the banks of Loch Ness. As he walked, he heard water splashing. Jergens turned and saw...well, the tape speaks for itself."

Finn held up a videotape. He turned to Melba Frye. "May I use your VCR?"

"Go ahead," she said.

Finn popped the tape into a VCR next to a TV in the corner of the meeting room.

"Jergens had his tape rolling when he saw the monster," Finn said.

Skilly and Muldew stared at the TV. Static filled the screen. Then they saw a path alongside a pretty lake. Trees lined one side. The smooth surface of the water was on the other side of the path. Patches of fog covered the calm water. The image bobbed, as if the person shooting the video were walking.

"It's a pretty lake, isn't it?" Finn said.

"It is," Muldew agreed.

"What you're about to see isn't so pretty."

From the TV speakers came the sounds of splashing, then a low, growling roar. The image on the screen came to a halt. Then, slowly, the camera scanned across the lake.

Skilly and Muldew gasped. A huge, scaly creature was crawling from the lake! Its black body was about the size and shape of an elephant's. It had a long neck, like a giraffe. Instead of legs, it had flippers, like a walrus. The creature turned toward the camera. Its cold gray eyes went wide, then it opened its jaws and roared.

The tape stopped. Snow filled the screen.

"That's when Wolfie shut off the camera and ran," Finn said. "I can't say that I blame him."

Skilly looked at the German man. Jergens was still reading his newspaper. He stifled a yawn.

"That's an amazing tape," Muldew said. "Can we take it? I'm sure that the scientists in our lab would like to study it."

"Not on your life," Finn said, removing the tape from the machine. He held it tight. "This is the only copy in the world. It's straight out of Wolfie's video camera. I'm not about to let it get erased by 'accident' at the FBI." Finn began to yell. "The people have a right to know the truth!" he bellowed. "Monsters exist!" Finn turned to Melba Frye with a warm smile. "And that's why I want to show this tape on the C-NEWS network."

Skilly and Muldew shared a quick look. "After you broadcast the tape, what are you going to do with it?" Skilly asked Joe Finn.

Finn shrugged his shoulders. "Make copies. Sell 'em over the Internet. At one hundred dollars a tape, we stand to make a few bucks!"

Skilly and Muldew huddled with Melba Frye in the back of the room.

"I don't trust them," Skilly said. "I think the tape may be a fake."

"I agree," Muldew said. "But without studying it in the lab, we can't prove anything."

Melba Frye gave a smile. "Oh, yes, we can," she said. "You two may be the experts in monsters and UFOs. But I'm the expert in TV and video. And now I know that Finn isn't telling the truth!"

STOP HERE

DISCUSSION QUESTIONS

1. Why did Melba Frye ask Agents Skilly and Muldew for their help?

2. Do Skilly and Muldew know Joe Finn? What do they think of him? How does he feel about Skilly and Muldew?

3. How does Wolfgang Jergens act as "his" video is played? What does that tell you about him? What might it tell you about the tape?

4. How does Melba Frye know that Finn is lying? Think about his story. What details about it do not add up? (This one is tough!) Talk about the possible endings for this story.

Then continue reading to see if you were right.

Skilly and Muldew shared a satisfied look. Melba Frye had pointed out that there was no way that a videotape shot on a European video camera would play on a VCR made to be used in America. Europeans and Americans use different types of videotape!

When his lie was pointed out to him, Finn blushed with embarrassment.

"Well, okay, so I told a little lie," Finn admitted. "Jergens didn't shoot that tape. He's just a guy I met on a tour bus yesterday. The fact is, I shot the video of the Loch Ness monster with my own camera. But who would believe a guy like me?"

"Not me," Melba Frye said. "But I will trust you if you let the FBI examine that tape, to see if it's a fake. If they say the monster is real, then we'll put it on the air."

Finn grabbed the tape and held it close. "No way!" he said.

"Do you have something to hide?" Skilly asked.

"Maybe I do, and maybe I don't," Finn said. He smiled suddenly. "And maybe they'll show this tape on the Fox Network!" he said.

HEX FILE #N286-1
"Star Light, Star Bright"

Before Reading

BUILDING BACKGROUND

Ask astronomy buffs to tell the rest of the class what constellations are. They should point out that constellations are patterns in the stars, and that people in ancient times told stories about the figures they imagined seeing in the patterns.

Tell students that one of the most easily spied constellations is the Big Dipper. Point out that the base of the Big Dipper points to the North Star, also called the Pole Star. See if any student knows the significance of the North Star for travelers.

If no student can answer, tell the class that it's called the North Star since the star is always in the northern sky, hovering over the North Pole. Tell students that, unlike the rest of the stars, the North Pole stays fixed in one place in the night sky. The rest of the stars move like the moon across the sky each night. For that reason, for thousands of years people have used the North Star to navigate. Ask students to keep this fact in mind as they read the story.

READING STRATEGY FOCUS: MAKING INFERENCES

An inference is a reasonable guess based on text clues as well as the reader's own knowledge and experience. Ask students to make an inference about Roid's character as they read the story.

VOCABULARY

Here are words your students will encounter in this story, along with their appropriate meanings:

community—a group of people living close together

constellation—a pattern seen in a group of stars

contract—a legal agreement

evidence—something that proves a fact is true

fictional—made up, imaginary

headquarters—the home office

hovering—floating in air

leisure—relaxation, playing

receipt—a paper slip that records a sale

retirement—to be no longer working

riveted—fixed upon

scientifically—having to do with science and science facts

similar—alike

suspicious—not trusting

After Reading

TALK ABOUT IT

What conclusions can students make about the photos in Roid's album?

WRITE ABOUT IT

Have students work in teams to do research on constellations. Have each team pick a constellation and prepare a short presentation or skit based on the myths and legends of the figure in their constellation.

HEX FILE #N286-1
"Star Light, Star Bright"

○ ○ ○ ○ ○ ○ ○ ○ ○ ○ ○

In this story, Skilly and Muldew meet up with an old friend who has a new trick up his sleeve.

○ ○ ○ ○ ○ ○ ○ ○ ○ ○ ○

"Well, well, well," Muldew said. "If it isn't our old friend Andy Roid."

FBI Agents Skilly and Muldew were visiting "Leisure Acres," a retirement community for the rich.

Earlier that day, the FBI agents had gotten a tip that something fishy was going on at Leisure Acres. As Skilly and Muldew drove up to the gates of the community, they saw hundreds of golf carts parked outside a building.

"What's going on there?" Skilly asked the security guard manning the gates.

"That's the community center," the guard explained. "There's a meeting. A guy is selling real estate on Mars, or something like that."

Skilly and Muldew parked behind the golf carts and headed into the community center. In the main room, dozens of rosy-cheeked, gray-haired people sat at tables. Their eyes were riveted on a younger man who stood at the head of the room, a microphone in his hand.

The man was Andy Roid. A few months earlier, Skilly and Muldew had exposed Roid as a liar. Roid had been speaking at a convention of science fiction fans. He had been trying to sell his fictional story of being kidnapped by aliens as a true story. Skilly and Muldew proved to the audience that Roid's story was scientifically impossible.

Now, here he was, telling senior citizens about his friendship with space aliens. Only this time, Roid was trying to sell more than just books!

"Life on the planet Altair is like heaven," Roid was saying. "The aliens who live there never fight. Each day is warm and sunny, and gentle breezes blow."

"Do they get cable?" asked one old-timer.

"There is no TV on Altair," Roid said. The crowd murmured at this.

"And you won't miss it! Life on Altair is so perfect that no one ever gets bored or lonely."

"I don't know," the old man grumbled. "I can't get through the night without my dose of 'Wheel of Fortune.'"

Muldew and Skilly watched in anger as Roid continued to describe the joys of life on Altair. At the end of his talk, Roid held up a receipt book.

"I have been sent here by the people of Altair, to sell you houses on their distant planet," Roid said. "Make your down payment today. Just give me a check for whatever amount you can afford."

An hour later, the last of the retirees had handed Roid a check and headed into the sunset. Altair sat at the table counting his money. Skilly and Muldew stepped up to him.

"I've seen dishonest people before," Muldew said. "But you are the worst. How dare you take advantage of those old folks?"

Roid turned red with anger. "You two, again!" he snapped. "I'm not taking advantage of anyone. I've been sent here by the aliens on the planet Altair. They want to offer their planet as a final resting place for old folks."

"Don't lie to us," Skilly said. "Now, tear up all of those checks. You're not going to make a dime off of these old-timers."

"I don't suppose you have proof that you've met with aliens?" Muldew added.

Roid got a sneaky smile on his face. "As a matter of fact, I do," he said. Roid took a photo album from his briefcase. "I took these pictures when the aliens visited me last January," Roid said.

Skilly opened the album. The first photo showed the night sky. Skilly recognized the constellation Orion in the middle of the sky. "Hold on," she said. "There's something funny here."

"What?" Muldew asked.

"There's an extra star in Orion."

Roid shook his head. "That's not a star. That's a space ship," he said. "The aliens were traveling from their home planet, which is in the constellation of Orion. I took that photo at around midnight. A few minutes later...."

Roid flipped to the next page of the album. Skilly gasped. The photo showed a giant flying saucer hovering over the ground. In the next photo, two aliens with gray skin and dark eyes stood next to the saucer, waving to the camera.

"I explained to my alien friends the trouble I had with you two before,"

Roid said. "They agreed to pose for pictures this time."

"That was nice of them," Muldew muttered.

In the next picture, the aliens and Roid sat around a kitchen table playing cards. "I had a good time catching up on old times with my friends from Altair," Roid said. "While we were playing Crazy Eights, the aliens kept telling me how beautiful their planet is. That's when I got the idea of selling real estate there."

In the next photo, the aliens and Roid were hard at work, writing something on a piece of paper. "There we are, writing the basic sales contract," Roid explained.

In the next photo, the aliens and Roid stood alongside the flying saucer shaking hands. "There we are after we made our agreement," Roid said. "I wanted them to stay and help me sell the real estate, but the aliens were eager to return home."

The last photo was similar to the first. The space ship, barely visible as a speck of light against the pitch-dark sky, was flying back into the heart of the constellation Orion.

"And there they go, back home." Roid sat back with confidence. "Maybe this time you'll believe me," he said.

"Maybe we won't," Muldew said. "You could have faked those photos."

"You are so suspicious," Roid said. "The fact is, it's your word against mine." Roid waved a handful of checks under Muldew's nose. "And these people are more eager to believe me than you."

Skilly studied the last photo. "Maybe I believe you, too," she said. Muldew looked at his partner, shocked.

"Why, thank you," Roid said. "It's good to see that one of you has the common sense to believe your own eyes."

"I've got one question," Skilly said. "How long did you visit with the aliens the night you took these pictures?"

Roid thought it over. "Let's see, we played cards for about an hour, then I got my idea about selling real estate. We worked out the details for a few more hours. I'd say we were together about three hours all together. Why?"

Skilly smiled. "Because now I know that you're not telling the truth."

"What?" Roid sputtered. "How can you say that? There's the evidence! Don't you believe your own eyes?"

"Yes, I do," Skilly said. She showed the last photo to Muldew. "And I'll bet my partner will see the light, too."

Muldew looked at the photo. Then he too smiled. "Roid, if you don't

54

tear up those checks right now, we're going to arrest you for fraud," he said. "You gave us the proof yourself!"

STOP HERE

Discussion Questions

1. *Why did Agents Skilly and Muldew visit Leisure Acres?*

2. *What is Andy Roid trying to sell the people who live at Leisure Acres? Is he successful? How do you know?*

3. *What evidence does Roid have to prove that his story is true? Describe it.*

4. *How does Skilly figure out that Roid is lying? What about his story doesn't hold up to the light? Talk about the possible endings for this story.*

Now continue reading to see if you were right.

Skilly pointed out that in the first picture, the constellation Orion was in the middle of the sky. That's where it would be around midnight in January.

But the last photo, supposedly taken three hours later, still showed Orion in the middle of the dark sky. By that time, the stars would have moved so much that Orion would be out of the sky!

"Did I say that photo was them leaving?" Roid said, sweating. "My mistake! I actually took two photos of them arriving!"

"Look, Roid," Muldew said. "We've already caught you in one lie. We can play this two ways. You can come with us to headquarters so we can study those photos more closely. If we find they are fakes, you're going to jail for a long, long time."

Roid gave a weak smile.

"What's the other way we can play it?" he asked.

"I think you know the answer to that," Skilly said.

Roid sighed, then began tearing up the checks he had collected.

"Wolf 'n' the Hood"

Before Reading

BUILDING BACKGROUND

Tell students that this story is a modern retelling of "Little Red Riding Hood" that pokes fun at the original story.

READING STRATEGY FOCUS: EXPLORING CHARACTERS AND SETTING

Have a volunteer tell the original version of the fairy tale. List the story's main characters and setting on the board:

Characters:

- Little Red Hiding Hood
- Wolf
- Grandma

Setting: Grandma's house in the woods

Point out that this version of the story is realistic, and there are no talking animals. Have students brainstorm how the story of Little Red Riding Hood could be told using real people. How would each of the three main characters be updated? Then read the story.

VOCABULARY

Here are words your students will encounter in this story, along with their appropriate meanings:

condo—an apartment

contagious—catching

lunged—made a swift move

scrambled—moved quickly

After Reading

TALK ABOUT IT

Discuss how the characters in this story stand the original characters on their heads:

- Riding Hood: Instead of being an innocent little girl, she's a confident, independent doctor.
- Grandma: Instead of being a weak old woman, she's an avid football fan.
- Wolf: Instead of being a dangerous animal who wants to eat Riding Hood, Wolf is a timid man with a crush on Riding Hood.

WRITE ABOUT IT

Let students pick a favorite fairy tale and update it in the same way, turning the characters into real people and making them the opposite of their original personalities. Have students write stories updating the fairy tales.

"Wolf 'n' the Hood"

○ ○ ○ ○ ○ ○ ○ ○ ○ ○

In this "fractured fairy tale," you'll meet a
very different Little Red Riding Hood.

○ ○ ○ ○ ○ ○ ○ ○ ○ ○

Dr. L. R. "Red" Hood was a very busy woman. When she wasn't busy curing sick people at the Mother Goose Memorial Medical Center, Red was working out in the gym. Her favorite sport was kickboxing.

"She works too hard," people would say, as they watched Red knock the stuffing out of a punching bag. "She's got to learn to relax. What she needs is a boyfriend."

In fact, dozens of doctors had asked Red out on dates. She always said, "No, thanks." Red was too busy to think about unimportant things like a boyfriend. Work and kickboxing were the two most important things in Red's life...after her grandmother, that is.

Red had been raised by her grandmother. The old woman lived in a condo complex called "The Woods." Every Sunday, Red went to her grandmother's for dinner. (Red always brought the dinner, since her grandmother didn't know how to cook.)

One Friday, when Red was at the gym, the phone in her office rang.

Arnie Wolf, a new janitor at the medical center, was in the office cleaning up. As the phone rang, Wolf looked around. The room was empty, so Wolf set down the trash can and picked up the phone.

"Hello," Wolf shyly said.

"Hi," Grandmother barked. "Is Red there?"

"Who?" Wolf asked.

"Dr. Hood!" Grandmother said. "This is her old granny."

"I'm sorry," Wolf said, "but no one is here at the moment."

"Humph." Grandmother said. "Give her a message, will you?" Wolf scrambled for a pencil and paper. "Tell her I scored a ticket to the Bears game on Sunday," Grandmother said. "I'm going to have to miss our regular dinner."

"You're going to have to miss Sunday dinner," Wolf said, writing a note. "Got it. I'll give her the message."

As he hung up, the door opened. Wolf looked up and gasped. The most beautiful woman he had ever seen stood in the doorway, drying her hair with a towel. A name tag on her jacket read "Dr. Hood."

"Who are you?" Red asked Wolf. The poor man was too stunned to speak.

"I'm a...I'm a...I'm a...." he stammered.

"You're a what?" Red asked.

"Janitor," Wolf croaked as he stumbled out of her office.

Later that night, Wolf sat in the cafeteria with Clark, his best janitor buddy.

"Dr. Hood is so beautiful," Wolf said.

"Forget about it!" Clark said. "Everyone knows that she won't go out with good-looking doctors. What makes you think she'd look twice at a guy like you?"

Wolf shrugged his shoulders. "Why not? She seemed to like janitors."

"Ha!" Clark laughed. "The only things Dr. Hood likes are her job, kickboxing, and her old grandma, in that order."

"Her grandmother!" Wolf gasped, remembering the message he had forgotten to give. He jumped to his feet, ready to head to Dr. Hood's office.

Then he stopped. He had an idea. If his idea worked, Arnie Wolf thought it might help him to win the heart of Dr. L. R. Hood.

That Sunday, Red's grandmother stepped out the door of her condo. She wore a Bears sweatshirt and held a big foam rubber hand with "We're #1!" printed on it.

Grandmother locked her front door, then looked around to make sure no one was watching. She hid the key under her mat, then walked off, whistling the Bears' fight song.

Arnie Wolf, watching from around the corner, saw his chance. He sneaked up to the door and took the key from under the mat. Using the key, Wolf let himself into Grandmother's condo.

Later that afternoon, Red came to the door of the condo carrying a paper bag filled with Chinese food. She bent over to get the key hidden under the mat. Red was surprised to see that the key was missing. She tried the front door. It was open.

"That's odd," Red told herself as she entered her grandmother's condo. "Grandma!" she called out. "Are you home?"

"I'm in the—" a low voice began. Red heard the voice give a little cough, then continue. "I'm in the bedroom."

Very curious now, and just a little worried, Red set down the food. She headed into the bedroom. What she saw made Red gasp in surprise.

The room was dark. The curtains were shut, and the only light came from a TV tuned to a football game. Through the shadows, Red could see somebody lying in her grandmother's bed, with the covers pulled all the way up. The person in the bed wore her grandmother's baseball cap, its bill pulled low. Only a pair of eyes could be seen.

"Grandma, are you all right?" Red gasped.

"Stay back!" the harsh voice called. Red stopped in her tracks. "I have a touch of the flu," the voice continued. "It's very contagious."

"Hmmm," Red said, suspicious. "I haven't heard of any flu bugs going around."

"Did I say flu?" the voice croaked. "I meant a cold." With that, Red's "grandmother" gave a harsh sneeze.

"You sound terrible," Red said. "You need help. Let me bring you a bowl of soup."

"I'll be fine!" "Grandmother" said. "Er—speaking of help, there's someone I want to tell you about."

"Who?" Red asked.

"His name is Wolf," "Grandmother" said. "I met him at your office. What a smart young man! And kind! He helped me cross the street."

Red narrowed her eyes. "When were you at my office?"

"Uh…Tuesday?" "Grandmother" said. "When you were in the gym. I stopped by just to say hello. Anyway, as I say, I met Arnie Wolf, who is a very handsome, very funny janitor—"

Red smiled as she stared at her "grandmother." "You know, I never noticed this before, but what big eyes you have."

"Uh…the better to see you with?" "Grandmother" replied.

"And what big, hairy knuckles you have," Red said. The hands disappeared under the blankets.

"The better to hold on to you, my dear," "Grandmother" said.

"Oh, yeah?" Red said. "Well, you better hold on to that blanket!"

With that, Red grabbed the end of the blanket and gave a mighty tug. The blanket flew off the bed.

Huddled on the mattress was Arnie Wolf.

"I thought so!" Red yelled. She crouched in a kickboxing pose. Wolf scrambled back. "Before I beat you up," Red yelled, "you had better tell me what you did to my grandmother. Now!"

STOP HERE

DISCUSSION QUESTIONS

1. *What are the most important things in Red's life?*

2. *How does Wolf meet Red? How does he feel when he meets her? How do you know?*

3. *Where does Red's grandmother go on Sunday? What does Wolf do that day? What is his plan?*

4. *What do you think will happen next? Summarize the story so far, then make a prediction.*

Now continue reading to see if you were right.

"Now, now, take it easy!" Wolf said, as he jumped from the bed. "Your grandmother is fine!"

"Where is she?" Red demanded.

"At the Bears game!" Wolf said. "She left a message for you the other day. I—er—forgot to tell you."

"Don't give me that," Red said. "Everyone knows that Grandmother loves baseball, not football!"

Red lunged for Wolf. He jumped out of the way, tripped, and fell to the floor. Red crouched, ready to leap on him.

"Look!" Wolf said, pointing to the football game on the TV. "I told you!"

Red looked at the TV. The picture showed the crowd celebrating a touchdown. There, in the middle of the picture, was Red's grandmother. She had painted her face orange, and was waving the big foam rubber hand.

Red turned to Wolf, a confused look on her face. "If she's at the game, what are you doing here?"

Wolf explained what had happened. "I thought if your grandmother put in a good word for me, then you might like me."

"That's sweet," Red said, as she led Wolf to the door of the condo. "No one's ever gone to this much trouble to impress me."

"Did it work?" Wolf asked. "Will you go out with a sweet man like me?"

"You haven't asked me yet."

Wolf swallowed hard and worked up his courage. "Dr. Hood," he asked, "Will you go out with me?"

Hood smiled sweetly.

"No, thanks," she said, shutting the door on Wolf's face.

"Bears in the City"

BUILDING BACKGROUND

This story imagines the Three Bears on vacation in New York City and Goldilocks as a little con artist who breaks into their room.

First, have a volunteer retell the Goldilocks fairy tale. Next, ask students if they have ever visited New York City. Brainstorm a list of attractions in New York that tourists visit. Tell students that in this story, the Three Bears visit New York. Have students predict what they think will happen.

READING STRATEGY FOCUS: MAKING CONNECTIONS

Good readers make connections between a story and their own lives. For instance, a character may remind the reader of someone he or she knows. Ask students to think about people or situations in their own lives that they're reminded of as they read this story.

VOCABULARY

Here are words your students will encounter in this story, along with their appropriate meanings:

luggage—*suitcases*

romance—*a love story*

sarcastically—*not seriously*

After Reading

TALK ABOUT IT

Ask students why they think the Three Bears gave Goldie a second chance. Then ask students what they would have done.

WRITE ABOUT IT

Have students plan a tour of three places in their community. Have them write a descriptive paragraph about the three places that will make visitors want to visit.

"Bears in the City"

◦ ◦ ◦ ◦ ◦ ◦ ◦ ◦ ◦ ◦ ◦ ◦

The Three Bears' visit to New York City is full of surprises.

◦ ◦ ◦ ◦ ◦ ◦ ◦ ◦ ◦ ◦ ◦ ◦

"My, but it's a big town," Mama Bear said. She stood by the window of the hotel room, looking at the busy street below. She had a worried look on her furry face. "I hope we don't get lost."

"Now, Mama, don't worry," said Papa Bear. He was looking at a colorful map. "It's easy to find your way around, if you just follow the map," he said.

"I want to go to the zoo!" whined Baby Bear.

"All in good time," said Papa Bear. "First we're going to visit the top of the Empire State Building." Papa Bear began loading his video camera, tapes, and batteries into a backpack. "Then we're going to some museums. Then we're visiting the Stock Exchange. Then—"

"But I want to look at some animals!" Baby Bear cried.

"Dear, you can see all sorts of animals back in the forest," Mama Bear said. "Since we're in the big city, let's see how people live."

Baby Bear gave a disappointed little growl. Their hotel room was small. The noise of honking cars and roaring traffic hurt his ears. If this was how people lived, he thought, they could have it.

"Ready troops?" Papa Bear said. "Let's hit the streets!"

The Three Bears headed out of the hotel room for their first day of vacation in New York City.

Mama Bear and Papa Bear were so excited that they didn't notice that Papa Bear had left his map on the bed.

Meanwhile, in the hotel lobby, a cute little girl with curly blonde hair watched people come and go. When the Three Bears got off the elevator, the little girl sat up.

"Bears in a hotel?" she thought. "That's a new one."

Goldie Lox (that was the girl's name) listened as Papa Bear left his room key at the front desk. "We're going to be coming back late," Papa Bear told the clerk.

"Your key will be waiting," the clerk said. He hung the key on a rack.

Goldie watched as the Three Bears marched out the door and away. Then she went to the front desk.

"Do you have any messages for me?" Goldie asked the clerk in her sweetest, most innocent voice. "My name is Lox. Goldie Lox."

"Hmmm. There are no messages here," the clerk said. "Maybe there are some in our message center in the back room."

"Could you check?" Goldie asked. The clerk turned and went into the back room. He came out a few seconds later.

"I'm sorry, miss," the clerk said. "There are no messages for—"

The clerk stopped. Goldie was gone. The clerk shrugged his shoulders, then returned to work.

He didn't notice that something else was gone…the key to the Three Bears' room.

"Darn it!" Goldie said. She was in the Three Bears' room, looking through their stuff. Goldie had found nothing but some jars of honey and Papa Bear's map. Being Bears, the three of them hadn't even packed clothes.

Goldie was tired, so she decided to take a minute to rest. She headed to a big chair in the corner and sat down.

"Who was this chair made for?" Goldie asked herself as she sank into the cushions. "It's way too soft." Goldie pulled herself from the chair and sat in another one near a writing desk.

"Ouch!" Goldie said. "This is way too hard." She spied another chair near the TV. She sat down.

"Ahhh," Goldie said. "This one is just right."

Goldie turned on the TV. Words on the screen told her that she'd have to pay money for every movie she watched. Goldie ignored the words and changed the channel to a movie.

Bullets flew on the screen. Bombs fell. Goldie watched the war movie for a few minutes. "This is way too violent," she said, changing channels.

The next movie was a romance. Goldie watched for a minute or two as a couple kissed. "This movie is way too sappy," she said, changing channels. This time, a comedy came on the TV.

"Ahhh," Goldie said. "This one is just right."

By now, Goldie was feeling hungry. She opened the small refrigerator in the room. Inside it, she saw three bags of snacks: peanuts, pretzels, and chips. Goldie was about to open the peanuts, when she got an idea.

"Why am I eating this junk?" Goldie said. "I could order room service!"

It was late at night by the time the Three Bears made it back to their hotel. Their feet were sore, their eyelids were heavy, and their stomachs growled.

"I want the key to our room," Papa Bear told the clerk. "We're the Three Bears."

The clerk turned to the rack. A worried look crossed his face. "Hmmm. Your key seems to be missing."

"Oh, that's perfect," Baby Bear groaned.

"Shhh!" Mama Bear said, quieting her son.

"Here is a spare key," the clerk said, handing it to Papa Bear. "Would you like a wake-up call in the morning?"

Papa Bear growled and shook his head, as he led Mama Bear and Baby Bear to the elevators.

The day had not gone well for the Three Bears. Without a map, they got in a subway heading in the wrong direction. Instead of going to the Empire State Building, they ended up way out in Brooklyn. Of course, no one in Brooklyn had ever seen bears before, at least not bears outside of cages. Whenever the Bears stopped someone to ask directions, the person would scream and run away. Finally, after many hours of wandering under the hot sun, the Three Bears had walked all the way back to their hotel.

"Gee, that was a fun way to spend the first day of our vacation," Baby Bear said, sarcastically, as they walked down the hallway.

"I don't want to hear it," Papa Bear grumbled as he unlocked the door to their room. "I just want to take a hot bath and relax."

Papa Bear opened the door—then froze. He saw their luggage spread out on the floor.

"Oh, no!" Papa Bear said. "Someone's been looking though my suitcase!"

"And someone's been looking in my suitcase," Mama Bear said.

"And someone's been looking in my suitcase," Baby Bear whined, "And they took all of my honey!"

Papa Bear tiptoed into the room. He stepped on a piece of paper that had been slipped under the door. Papa Bear picked up the paper and gasped.

"What's wrong?" Mama Bear asked.

"It's a bill from the hotel!" Papa Bear said. "Someone's been charging movies to our room! And someone's been making long distance phone calls! And someone's been ordering porridge from room service!"

Baby Bear stared at his bed. A head of blonde curls rested on the pillow.

"And that someone is still here!" Baby Bear said.

 64

STOP HERE

DISCUSSION QUESTIONS

1. *Why are the Bears in the big city?*

2. *Why do you think Goldie was in the hotel lobby? What does Goldie do after the Bears leave?*

3. *What happens to the Bears over the course of the day?*

4. *What do you think will happen next? Think about the traditional version of "Goldilocks and the Three Bears." Then review the story so far. Make a prediction about how it will turn out.*

Now continue reading to see if you were right.

Mama Bear screamed with fear. Goldie sat up, half asleep. She saw Papa Bear grab the telephone. Goldie started to get out of the bed.

"Don't move!" Papa Bear said.

"What are you going to do?" Goldie asked.

"What do you think?" Papa Bear said. "I'm calling the cops! You broke into our room, went through our stuff, charged food to my credit card...."

Goldie sobbed. "I'm sorry," she said. "I just get so tired and hungry. The city is so big, and I'm so small."

"Do you live here?" Mama Bear asked Goldie.

Goldie nodded. "I was born and raised in New York. But I'm too young to have a job, and I need money to survive."

"Hmmm," Baby Bear said. "Do you know how to get to the zoo?"

"Yes," Goldie asked.

"How about the Empire State Building?" Mama Bear asked.

"Of course," Goldie replied.

"Do you know the directions to the Stock Exchange?" Papa Bear asked.

"Sure I do," Goldie said. "Why do you ask?"

Papa Bear smiled at Mama Bear. She smiled back. "I just figured out how you can pay us back," Papa Bear said.

And that's how "Goldie Lox Big Apple Tours" got its start. If you're ever in New York, and a bear or a deer or a badger stops to ask you for directions, just tell them to call GOL-D-LOX and ask for the grand tour.

Tell them to say the Three Bears sent you.

"Huffing and Puffing"

Before Reading

BUILDING BACKGROUND

"I'll huff and I'll puff and I'll blow your house down!" Ask students if they can name which fairy tale that famous line of dialogue is from. Have a volunteer retell the story of "The Three Little Pigs."

Tell students that many fables and fairy tales have a "moral," that is, a simple lesson that can be expressed in a sentence or two. ("Honesty is the best policy," "A bird in hand is worth two in the bush," etc.)

Discuss with the class a possible moral for the original version of "The Three Little Pigs." Possible morals would be "Be prepared," or "Always learn from your mistakes."

READING STRATEGY FOCUS: SUMMARIZING

Have students think about how they would summarize this story as they read. Remind them that in a summary, you state in a few sentences the major events of the story. Then read the story.

VOCABULARY

Here are words your students will encounter in this story, along with their appropriate meanings:

blizzard—*big snowstorm*

construction—*building*

discount—*special sale price*

inquiring—*curious*

rebuilding—*to knock a building down and build it again*

shivering—*trembling with cold*

After Reading

TALK ABOUT IT

Return to your discussion of fairy tale morals and the students' suggestions for a moral to the story of the Three Pigs. Ask students if the moral of this version of the story is the same as the moral of the original story of the Three Pigs.

WRITE ABOUT IT

Challenge students to write a sequel to this version of the Three Pigs. Ask: What might happen to the pigs' house of sand? Where will the pigs go after that? How might they run into the Big Bad Wolf? Let students share their sequels with the class.

"Huffing and Puffing"

The Three Pigs are expert carpenters, but is that enough?

"It looks like a winter storm is ready to strike," the TV Weather Person said. "A blizzard is moving through. That means high winds will be huffing and puffing all night long!"

The three pigs, Wilbur, Gordy, and Babe, were having dinner in front of the TV as the Weather Person gave his prediction.

"Looks like a big storm is brewing," Wilbur said.

"Yep," said his brother, Gordy. "A big storm. Can't say that I like storms."

"Nor do I," said the third brother, Babe. "It's a good thing our house is made out of straw. A straw house is built to last."

The phone rang. Wilbur answered it.

"Hello," said a voice over the line. "I'm calling on behalf of B.B. Wolf's Home Construction Company. Could I speak to Mr. Pig, Please?"

"This is Pig," Wilbur gruffly said.

"Who is it?" Gordy asked Wilbur.

"Some salesperson," Wilbur told his brother. "They always call when we're eating dinner." He turned back to the phone. "What are you selling?" Wilbur asked.

"Mr. Pig, have you considered fixing up your house?" the caller asked.

"No," Wilbur said. "Why should I?"

"This winter weather can ruin the finest homes," the salesperson said. "We are offering a special discount on rebuilding your home with bricks."

"Bricks?" Wilbur laughed. "Who needs bricks? We built this house with our own trotters using straw. Have you ever seen a straw house blown down?"

"No," the salesperson said. "In fact, I've never seen a straw house, period."

"That's your problem, not mine!" With that, Wilbur hung up the phone. "I can't believe someone would try to tell *me* how to build a house," Wilbur grumbled. He sat down in front of the TV with his two brothers. Outside, the wind howled.

It was true: the three pigs were expert carpenters. They could make a three-bedroom house out of playing cards and shoestring. They could make a four-car garage out of dryer lint and chewed bubble gum. The problem was, for all of their skill as carpenters, the pigs were lousy at planning. They had no idea what materials to use. Worst of all, they never learned from their mistakes.

The next morning, the three pigs woke up shivering in the cold. Snow three feet deep covered the ground. Sticking out of the snow were thousands of stalks of straw. It was all that was left of their house.

"Hmmm," Gordy said, as he looked over the remains of their house. "Maybe straw wasn't the best building material to use, after all."

"Maybe it wasn't," Wilbur agreed. "But what could be better than straw?"

"You want to know what's better than straw?" Babe said. He reached down and pulled a twig from the snow. "Sticks!"

All winter the pigs worked on their house. They gathered sticks. They wove them together to build walls and a roof. They even used sticks to make a fireplace and chimney—although they had the good sense not to use it.

Finally, just as the snow was melting, the house of sticks was ready. The proud pigs moved in.

That night, the pigs watched the Weather Channel on TV.

"Looks like a big twister is blowing through," the Weather Person said. "It's going to be huffing and puffing all night long!"

"Makes you feel safe and sound, knowing that you live in a house of sticks, huh, boys?" Wilbur said. His brothers nodded in agreement.

That night, a storm hit. Just as the Weather Person had predicted, the wind huffed and puffed and howled outside the pigs' new house.

The next morning, there was no house—just a pile of sticks. The pigs stood in the middle of what was left of their home, scratching their heads.

"Well, I'll be a monkey's uncle," Wilbur said. "We tried straw. We tried sticks. What do we try next?"

The phone started to ring. It took the pigs a few minutes of digging through the rubble before Babe finally found the phone.

"Hello," Babe said into the phone.

"Hello," said a voice. "I'm calling on behalf of B.B. Wolf's Home Construction Company. We're offering a spring special. We can remodel your house using bricks. Are you interested?"

Babe put the phone down and turned to his brothers. "Hey, fellows," he said, "I think I have the answer to our problem!"

STOP HERE

DISCUSSION QUESTIONS

1. *What are the three pigs doing as the story starts?*

2. *Who calls the three pigs? What does the person offer? How do the pigs respond?*

3. *What happens to the pigs and their houses? What is the pigs' greatest talent? What is their weakness?*

4. *What do you think will happen next? Make a prediction.*

Then continue reading to see if you were right.

Later that day, the pigs paid a visit to B.B. Wolf, the president of B.B. Wolf's Home Construction Company.

"What can I do for you boys?" Wolf asked as the three pigs sat down in front of his big, solid desk.

"Mr. Wolf, we are expert carpenters," Babe said. "We want to work for you."

"Call me Big-Bad," Wolf said, as he gave the pigs an inquiring glance. "Can you prove to me that you know how to build houses?"

The three pigs showed Wolf pictures of their houses made of straw and sticks. "Hmmm," Wolf said as he looked them over. "These are nice. I can't say I'd make a house out of straw or sticks. But if I did, I'd want it to look like this." Wolf set the pictures aside. "Tell you what I'm going to do. You three pigs come work for me. In exchange, I'll build a house of bricks just for you. How does that sound?"

"To tell you the truth, sir, we'd rather be paid with cash," Wilbur explained.

"We're saving up our money," Gordy said. "By the end of the summer we hope to save enough to move to Florida," Babe added. "Someplace warm, where the winter wind doesn't huff or puff."

A few months later, the three pigs had saved enough to move to Florida. The new house they built was on the beach outside Miami. Their first night there, the three pigs tuned in the Weather Channel.

"There's a big storm off the coast of Florida," the Weather Person said. "Looks like it could be a hurricane. The wind will be huffing and puffing."

"It sure makes you feel safe and sound to be living in a house made out of sand, doesn't it?" Babe said.

His brothers nodded in agreement.

"The Tortoise and the Hare and the Frog"

Before Reading

BUILDING BACKGROUND

Write the word "sequel" on the board. Ask a volunteer to define the word. (A sequel is a story about characters who have already appeared in another story.) Make a list of sequels students are familiar with, both in books and movies.

Ask students why some sequels are better than others. Hold a discussion on what makes a sequel work. Lead students to understand that a good sequel tells you more about characters that you already like, and doesn't just tell the same story over again.

READING STRATEGY FOCUS: MAKING PREDICTIONS

Tell students that this story is a sequel to the fairy tale "The Tortoise and the Hare." Let a volunteer tell the original story in his or her own words. Then have students predict what might happen in a sequel to the story. Point out that the title of this story includes a third character. Then read "The Tortoise and the Hare and the Frog."

VOCABULARY

Here are words your students will encounter in this story, along with their appropriate meanings:

bandage—cloth wrapped around an injury

determination—with a firm purpose

gnawing—chewing constantly

muscular—well-built

reflection—to see your own image, as in a mirror

regret—sadness caused by thinking about something lost

taunting—making fun of

waddle—awkward, swaying walk

After Reading

TALK ABOUT IT

"The Hare and the Tortoise and the Frog" is a sports story. Invite students to describe their favorite books and movies about sports. Encourage them to look for similarities in the stories they share.

WRITE ABOUT IT

Challenge students to write a short story or play about sports. If they need a story starter, suggest that students use their favorite athletes as characters, and base their stories on classic fables or fairy tales. Let students illustrate their stories and share their work with the rest of the class.

"The Tortoise and the Hare and the Frog"

○ ○ ○ ○ ○ ○ ○ ○ ○ ○ ○

Who is *really* the fastest runner in the forest?

○ ○ ○ ○ ○ ○ ○ ○ ○ ○ ○

Everyone knows the story of the Tortoise and the Hare. About how the Hare was the fastest animal in the forest, and the Tortoise was the slowest. How the Tortoise challenged the Hare to a race. How the Hare was so confident he would win that he stopped to rest just a few feet short of the finish line. And how the Hare fell asleep, allowing the Tortoise to win the race.

But do you know what happened to the Tortoise and the Hare *after* the race?

The Tortoise became a superstar. All of the other animals in the forest looked up to him. Mommy and daddy turtles told their kids to eat all of their insects, if they wanted to grow up to be big and fast like the Tortoise.

The Hare, on the other hand, was very upset after losing the race. He stopped running and started hanging out in the carrot patch all day long. The Hare put on a lot of weight. Every time the Hare saw the Tortoise followed by dozens of adoring fans, it would make him sad, then angry.

"I could have beaten that Tortoise," the Hare would say to anyone who would listen. "I had him right where I wanted him. If only I had stayed awake...."

Soon, the other rabbits got tired of hearing the Hare's sob story. The Hare found himself all alone in his corner of the carrot patch, gnawing on carrots and filled with regret.

To all appearances, the Tortoise was happy and the Hare was sad. But the truth was very different. The Tortoise was far from happy. In fact, he was scared.

In his heart of hearts, the Tortoise knew that he had been lucky to win the race against the Hare. He also knew that just about any other animal in the world could beat him in a race. The Tortoise was afraid that one day he'd have to race again. He knew he would lose, and his fame would disappear.

The Tortoise vowed to never race again.

One sunny day, the Tortoise showed up at the opening of a new pond. Hundreds of other turtles were there to see their hero.

"Thank you all for coming out," Mayor Turtle told the crowd. "It's great to see you all today. And I know you're glad to see your hero and mine...the Tortoise!"

The Tortoise waved as the young turtles cheered.

"Do you have anything to say to the youngsters, Mr. Tortoise?" Mayor Turtle asked.

"I sure do," the Tortoise said, in his slow and steady voice. "Kids, always eat your insects. And be sure to listen to your parents, they know best."

The young turtles cheered again. The Tortoise turned to crawl off the rock and into the water, when a voice in the back crowd croaked out:

"He's not so fast!"

The young turtles gasped and turned to see who had insulted their hero. The Tortoise turned, too. There, at the edge of the crowd, was a big, muscular Frog.

"Don't say that about the Tortoise!" one young turtle scolded the Frog. "He beat the Hare in a race! How did he do that if he's not fast?"

"If he's so fast, then why doesn't he race another animal?" the Frog replied.

"Because he's too busy," said another turtle.

"Do you think so?" said the Frog. "I think it's because he's chicken."

"He's not a chicken!" yelled a turtle. "He's the Tortoise!"

The Frog gave the Tortoise a cold-eyed stare. "Prove you're not a chicken," Frog said. "Race me. If you win, then I take it all back—you are the fastest animal around. If you lose, then I'm right—you were just lucky to beat the Hare." The Frog gave a slimy smile. "And if you refuse to race," he said, "then I'm doubly right. You're not fast...and you're a chicken."

The Tortoise felt the eyes of hundreds of young turtles on him. Could he let them down?

Late that night, the Hare as usual sat all alone in the carrot patch listening to the sad sounds of crickets chirping, munching on carrots.

"You know, if you eat enough carrots, pretty soon the carrots start eating you," said a familiar voice. The Hare turned. He saw the Tortoise standing nearby.

"I happen to like carrots," said the Hare, starting on a fresh one.

"You've put on a few pounds, haven't you?" the Tortoise said, looking at the Hare's big, soft belly.

"So what?" the Hare said. "I lost the big race. What difference does it make now?"

"I think about that race every day," the Tortoise said, sitting next to the Hare. "I know that you had me beat. I always wondered why you stopped to take a nap."

"Don't try to make me feel better," the Hare said. "I'm a loser. Everyone knows it."

"I don't think you're a loser," the Tortoise said. "If I did, I wouldn't be here." The Tortoise smiled at the Hare. "I need your help. I need the help of a winner."

The Tortoise explained what had happened at the pond. How the Frog had challenged him to a race. The Tortoise had to accept the challenge, or he'd never be able to look at his reflection in the pond again.

"So what do you want from me?" the Hare asked.

"The race is going to happen in two weeks," the Tortoise said. "In that time, I need you to teach me how to be fast. I need a trainer, and I can't think of anyone I'd rather learn from than you."

And so the Tortoise and the Hare began to work together. The Hare led the Tortoise on long runs in the morning. The Tortoise was slow at first. As the days wore on, he didn't get any faster.

In the afternoon, the Hare and the Tortoise did wind sprints together. The Tortoise moved his legs as fast as he could, but he never went faster than a slow waddle.

In the evening, the Hare showed the Tortoise some exercises to strengthen his legs. The Tortoise did his best, but he never got a step faster.

The Hare, on the other hand, was doing great. He started to lose weight. He stopped hanging out in the carrot patch all day and all night long. He got his speed back. Most important of all, the Hare began to feel much better about himself.

At last, the day of the big race arrived. Hundreds of animals lined the course. The Frog waited near the starting line, stretching his powerful leg muscles.

The Tortoise, however, was a no-show.

The Hare paced nervously, waiting for the Tortoise. After all of the hard work they had put in over the past two weeks, the Hare was eager for the Tortoise to race.

The race was supposed to start at two o'clock. Two came and went, but still there was no sign of the Tortoise.

Mayor Turtle was about to cancel the race and declare the Frog the winner, when a gasp came from the back of the crowd. The turtles parted, revealing the Tortoise at the edge of the crowd. His front left leg was wrapped in a bandage.

The Hare hopped over to the Tortoise. "Where have you been?" the Hare asked. "Let's go! The race is about to start."

"I can't race," the Tortoise moaned. "I pulled a muscle in my leg."

"Oh, no," groaned the Hare. "Not after all of that running and sprinting and stretching! Don't tell me we're going to miss the race."

"No, we're not," the Tortoise said. He nodded at the Hare, then said with a smile, "We're not missing the race. Because you are going to take my place."

DISCUSSION QUESTIONS

1. *What happened to the Hare after he lost the race to the Tortoise? What happened to the Tortoise after he won the race?*

2. *How does the Tortoise act when he is with other animals? How does he secretly feel?*

3. *What happens at the pond? Why does the Tortoise accept the challenge to race the Frog? What is the Tortoise's plan to win the race?*

4. *What do you think will happen next? Think about the traditional version of "The Tortoise and the Hare." Then review the story so far. Make a prediction about how it will turn out.*

Now continue reading to see if you were right.

Hundreds of animals lined the racecourse as the Frog and the Hare toed the starting line.

"Planning to stop for a nap?" the Frog asked, taunting the Hare.

"You won't be so lucky," replied the Hare with great determination.

"On your mark," Mayor Turtle called. The Hare and the Frog crouched. "Get set!" Mayor yelled. The Frog and the Hare leaned forward. "Go!"

The animals cheered as the Frog and the Hare leapt from the starting line. The two racers shot like arrows down the course and around the first turn. It was neck and neck.

Then, about one hundred yards from the finish line, the Hare pulled ahead. He could hear the Frog gasping for breath behind him. As he drew closer and closer to the finish line, the Hare could hear the cheers of the animals lining the course. He was going to win!

The Hare took a split second to glance over at a tree near the finish line. It was the same tree he rested under during his race with the Tortoise. It was the same shady spot where he had fallen asleep that day. It was the same place where he lost the race.

"Not this time!" thought the Hare. Then he stopped in his tracks.

There, hanging from a branch of the tree, was the Tortoise! Far below him was a pile of hard rocks. The Tortoise held on for dear life. Then the branch lurched, and the Tortoise began to drop to the rocks below.

Sproing!

Quick as a flash, the Hare jumped from the racecourse. With two mighty leaps, he soared through the air and grabbed the Tortoise just as he was about to fall onto the rocks. As the Hare and the Tortoise landed safely on the grass, the Frog hopped across the finish line, winning the race.

Later, the Hare and the Tortoise sat together in the shade of the tree, watching the Frog sign autographs.

"Why were you up in the tree?" the Hare asked.

"I wanted to see you win the race, and all of the other spots were taken," the Tortoise explained.

"How did you climb the tree?" the Hare asked. "I thought you had pulled a muscle."

The Tortoise blushed. "I told a little white lie," he said. "My leg is fine. I just wanted to give you the chance to win the race." The Tortoise sighed sadly. "Looks like I made you lose again," he said.

The Hare smiled and patted his new friend on the back. "You didn't make me lose," the Hare said. "Thanks to you, I'll never feel like a loser again."

"beanstalk.com"

Before Reading

BUILDING BACKGROUND

Tell students this story sets "Jack and the Beanstalk" in the days of the Internet stock bubble. Ask students if they know what happened to Internet stocks in the late nineties and during the early years of this decade. Point out that many, many people invested money in Internet companies. The stock prices in the companies climbed higher and higher, even though most of the companies made no money. Then people began to sell their shares in Internet companies. Very quickly, the stock prices dropped to almost nothing.

READING STRATEGY FOCUS: MAKING PREDICTIONS

Ask students to predict how a story titled "beanstalk.com" would update Jack and the Beanstalk for the Internet age. Then read the story.

After Reading

TALK ABOUT IT

Remind students about the predictions they made about this story. Were they correct?

WRITE ABOUT IT

Tell students that people who want to start a business first write a business plan to show investors. A good business plan will describe the following:

- The product: What goods or services will the company sell?
- The market: Who will buy the company's products or services? How will the business let people know that the goods and services are available?
- The costs: What will it cost to provide the goods and services? This includes the cost for materials and the salaries to be paid to employees.

- Profit and loss: The difference between what a company spends and what it earns is called a profit or loss. A company has a profit if it earns more than it spends. A company has a loss if it spends more than it earns. A business plan should show that the business will make a profit, not a loss.

Have students work in teams to invent businesses. Each group should make a written business plan. Let each team present its business plan to the class. Then decide, as a class, which business they would invest in.

VOCABULARY

Here are words your students will encounter in this story, along with their appropriate meanings:

antique—old and valuable

exchange—a trade

headquarters—the home office

polished—rubbed to make something look shiny and new

"beanstalk.com"

○ ○ ○ ○ ○ ○ ○ ○ ○ ○ ○ ○

In this version of "Jack and the Beanstalk," Jack buys stock instead of beans.

○ ○ ○ ○ ○ ○ ○ ○ ○ ○ ○ ○

"That's the last of our food," Grandpa said, emptying the box of corn flakes into a bowl.

"Don't worry, Grandpa," said young Jack. "We still have Bessie. She gives us all of the milk we need."

"People can't live on milk alone," Grandpa said. "We need real food. That's why I've decided to sell Bessie."

Jack was shocked. "You want to sell our cow?" he asked. "We can't sell Bessie! She's part of the family!"

"I don't like it either," Grandpa said. "But with the money we earn selling Bessie, we can buy seeds. We can plant the seeds and grow crops. We can sell the crops and buy more seeds. Get it?"

Jack nodded. He still didn't want to sell his pet cow, but he understood why he had to.

And that's how Jack and Bessie came to be on the road to the county fair that day. At the fair, Jack would sell Bessie to the highest bidder.

A fancy car zoomed past Jack and Bessie, then squealed to a halt. It backed up alongside Jack. The driver rolled down the window.

"Where did you get that cowbell?" the driver asked, his voice shaking with excitement. He was a man in an expensive suit. Jack looked at the old metal bell hanging from Bessie's neck and shrugged his shoulders.

"I don't know," Jack said. "Bessie has always worn it."

The driver stared at the bell. "Yes, by golly, that's an antique Dutch cowbell!" he said. "My name is Cook. I collect cowbells. I've been looking for one of those for years!"

"That's nice," Jack said. "I'm in kind of a hurry. I have to get my cow Bessie to the county fair. I need to sell her for money."

"Money?" Cook said. "Haven't you heard, my friend? Cash is trash!"

"What do you have that's better?" Jack asked.

Cook smiled. "I'm a stockbroker," he said. "Are you ready to make a deal?"

Two hours later, Jack was back home facing his Grandpa. The old man's face was red with anger.

"Stocks?" he said. "You traded our cow for a few shares of a company's stock?"

"No! That's the best part!" Jack said. He pointed out the window. Bessie stood grazing in the yard. "All the man wanted was Bessie's cowbell. In exchange for the bell, he gave me all of these."

Jack held pieces of paper. They were shares of stock in a new company called "beanstalk.com."

"This company is going to sell super-sized beans over the Internet," Jack explained. "It's going to be huge!"

"Bah!" Grandpa said. "You can't eat stocks and bonds! Tomorrow I'm going to take Bessie to the fair myself."

Just then the phone rang. Jack answered. On the other end was Cook the stockbroker.

"Hey, kid, have you checked the price of beanstalk.com lately?" he asked.

"No," Jack said.

"It's through the roof!" Cook said. "I could kick myself! I gave you enough stock that you control the company. Oh well, you win some and you lose some. That old cowbell of yours sold for a hundred grand on e-Bay. See you later."

Jack hung up the phone in a daze.

"What was that all about?" Grandpa asked.

"I'm not sure," Jack said. "But I think we're rich."

Sure enough, overnight Jack's stock in beanstalk.com was worth millions. Jack and his grandpa were able to buy any food they wanted. Jack built a new barn for Bessie, and gave her a fine collection of new cowbells to choose from.

Then, one day Jack got a letter in the mail. It was on nice paper. The return address, printed in gold ink, read "Phee, Fye, Foefum, Attorneys at Law." Jack opened the letter and read it, a worried look on his face.

"What's wrong?" Grandpa asked.

"It's a letter from lawyers for the Jolly Blue Giant Food Company," Jack said. "It says that beanstalk.com stole their idea for selling beans over the Internet. They are going to sue me for every cent I own!"

The letter invited Jack to come to the Jolly Blue Giant Company headquarters in the big city. The lawyers said that maybe they could make a deal. Jack had no choice. He packed his bags and headed to the big city.

Jack stood on the sidewalk outside of the Jolly Blue Giant headquarters. The building was so tall that its top floors were hidden in the clouds. Jack swallowed his fear, and entered the building. When he told the security guard who he was, the man sent Jack to a special elevator to take him straight to the top floor.

When Jack got off the elevator, he found himself in a waiting room. It was filled with antique furniture. A stern woman sat behind a desk. "You must be Jack," she snapped.

"I am," Jack said shyly.

The woman picked up the phone. "He's here," she said. Then she hung up the phone and glared at Jack. "Wait here."

Jack sat nervously on a sofa. He looked around. After about five minutes, a door opened. A very short man smoking a very big cigar stood in the door.

"Jack, I'm Ed Giant, president of the Jolly Blue Giant company," the man said. He gave a mean smile. "Step into my office."

DISCUSSION QUESTIONS

1. *Why does Grandpa send Jack and Bessie to the county fair?*

2. *Who does Jack meet on his way to the county fair? What kind of deal does the man offer Jack?*

3. *How does Grandpa react when Jack returns home? What happens to make Grandpa change his mind about Jack's deal?*

4. *Why does Jack visit the headquarters of the Jolly Blue Giant Company? Think about the original story of "Jack and the Beanstalk." Make a prediction about how you think this story will turn out.*

Now continue reading to see if you were right.

Jack was no match for Ed Giant.

He sat at one end of the table. Giant, along with his lawyers, sat at the other. Giant pointed out that his company had the money to take a lawsuit all the way to the Supreme Court. Jack had a simple choice to make. He could spend all of his money on lawyers, or he could agree to sell beanstalk.com to Jolly Blue Giant for very little money.

Jack agreed to sell.

Two months later, the Jolly Blue Giant Company announced that its Internet business, beanstalk.com, had lost millions of dollars trying to sell giant beans over the Internet. Two months after that, the Jolly Blue Giant shut down beanstalk.com. The value of the Jolly Blue Giant Company dropped till it was next to nothing.

Jack, on the other hand, still had all of the money he had earned selling Ed Giant his shares in beanstalk.com.

"I'm telling you, kid, you have a golden touch," Grandpa later told Jack, as Jack polished his antique cowbell collection. "How do you do it?"

Jack smiled, then patted Bessie on the side. "I started out down here on the farm. The next thing I knew, I was way up in the clouds, visiting the Jolly Blue Giant building. And you know what they say is the secret to making money on the stock market....'Buy low, sell high!'"